THE LEADERSHIP LIFE

JOHN MEROLA

The Leadership Life
by John Merola
Copyright ©2016 John Merola

ISBN: 9781633600393
For Worldwide Distribution

Printed in the U.S.A.

TABLE OF CONTENTS

INTRODUCTION

I enjoy talking about leadership. In case you haven't noticed, there are plenty of others who feel the same way. The subject of leadership fills bookstore shelves, is one of the most frequently searched words on the Internet, and receives profuse attention from the media. And rightly so. The subject of leadership has a profound and far-reaching effect on us all.

Leadership impact is found in all aspects of life as we know it, and is crucial to the success of virtually every institution one can think of. Marriage, family, education, economics, medicine, government, military, business, church, you name it, are all dependent upon leadership to function properly. Whether we examine the history of notable events, or consider the situations of news-grabbing current events, or even if our focus is more toward the future, the impact of leadership is central to the analysis of what is wrong or what is right about the world in which we live.

So, if we're going to talk about leadership, let's start with defining it. How would you define leadership? What are your initial thoughts? Does the word leadership conjure up primarily negative connotations for you, such as being under the command and control of another? Maybe you see leadership as a necessary evil to be tolerated, but certainly never to be celebrated? Maybe you think of leadership as something to avoid, because you don't want the responsibility or you have seen too many other leaders fail? Or perhaps, your outlook equates leadership with enjoying the privilege and stature that comes with being the boss?

Whatever the case, you probably will not find a one-size-fits-all version of leadership. The subject of leadership involves people and situations that are sometimes complex. The perspectives may vary, but because of the potential that leadership holds for producing good or harm, we do well to give it due consideration.

A simple Internet search presents us with countless leadership definitions that could keep us busy all day. They range from short and simple to lengthy and complex. I've read plenty of them, and just like most other things, there are some that I really like and there are some with which I just don't connect.

Here are a few that I find meaningful:

- *Leadership is influence, nothing more, nothing less.* – John Maxwell
- *Leaders are dealers in hope.* - Napoleon Bonaparte
- *If your actions inspire others to dream more, learn more, do more, and become more, you are a leader.* – John Quincy Adams
- *A process whereby an individual influences a group of individuals to achieve a common goal.* – Peter Northouse
- *Leadership is the capacity to transform dreams into reality.* – Warren Bennis

Leadership is highly significant and greatly

valued. It uniquely and overwhelmingly affects every aspect of life, and is essential for the success of any endeavor. It is a strangely intangible yet deeply felt dynamic that is universally attractive. There is an aching in the soul of humanity that longs for authentic leadership. We may not always know exactly how to define it, but we all seem to recognize it when we see it in action.

But the purpose of my writing isn't just to add my own leadership definition to the already long list. Rather it is to share my ongoing perspective on the subject of leadership from the Bible. After all, God is the truest and purest of leaders, so why not learn from the best?

Perhaps you see the Bible as only a religious book, a collection of moral teachings for the devout. Maybe you view it as a historical account of ancient life or as a treasury of wise sayings and prayers. Or maybe, like myself, you esteem the Bible as a carefully-crafted and divinely-inspired message for all people, filled with life, truth, and power from the very heart of God. The wisdom contained in the Scriptures remains relevant to all things in all generations, including leadership. Whatever your thoughts on the Bible, I trust you will find this book to be a useful resource for leading well.

Leadership isn't just a title or a position. It goes beyond simply a list of right behaviors or necessary attributes. It's more than merely a rank or a role that is assigned to some. I consider leadership to be a lifestyle, a calling to be embraced, and a cause to be upheld. That's why the title of my book is, *The Leadership Life*.

I wanted to write this book because I have been a student of leadership for many years. My interest in leadership grew so much that I decided to pursue a graduate degree in Organizational Leadership. I recently completed my degree, and I enjoyed the journey immensely. My extensive reading on leadership during the program furthered my desire not only to be a strong leader, but also to develop strong leaders.

Our world is in crisis, and searching for answers. Many people I encounter are fearful and confused about the future. They struggle to make sense of the condition of our world. As a Christian and as a minister, I feel compelled to offer biblically-sound teaching and practical wisdom for our generation. I believe the solutions we seek begin with building godly leaders.

Why should you be interested in leadership? Not only because it affects you, but because God also wants to use your life to affect others. Whether you like it or not, want it or not, believe it or not, as a follower of Christ your life is called to some degree to become an expression of His character, His nature, and His leadership.

God is love and light, authority and power, goodness and truth, wisdom and blessing. He is the source and the sustainer of all life. He is the judge, the ruler, the king, and the master of all creation. God is all of that and more, yet the most amazing thing is that He calls us to share in the wealth of who He is and what He does. When we receive His Spirit within us and upon us, we become positioned as stewards of His gifts and abilities in order to serve His purposes.

1 Peter 4:10 tells us, *Each of you should use whatever gift you have received to serve others, as faithful stewards of God's grace in its various forms.* Every follower of Christ is equipped to lead somehow by serving our families, businesses, teams, communities, churches, or any other realm where our abilities are needed.

Please don't misunderstand my meaning. I am not saying that everyone should go about giving orders and trying to take charge in every situation. I am not implying that leaders are always right or that they always know better than others. That is not my message at all, and that is not the heart of authentic leadership. I said that each of us is equipped to lead by serving.

The Leadership Life calls us to live humbly among others and for others, seeking opportunities to grow and to release the special qualities that have been invested in us. Each of us is a leader in the sense that we bear the image of God, and consequently have received something from Him that can benefit others. Each of us has value, and each of us can and should make a contribution to humanity. There is a leadership context to each of our lives, a time and a place for those abilities to be applied. Unless we step up and do our part, we all miss out on the good that might have been.

One of my favorite verses is 1 Timothy 1:12, where the Apostle Paul wrote, *I thank him that enabled me, even Christ Jesus our Lord, for that he counted me faithful, appointing me to his service.* Several things are at work here. First of all, Paul recognized that we are enabled and empowered through our association with Christ Jesus. Secondly, Paul reminded us that we are accountable to Christ for the gifts, callings, and purposes He has entrusted to us. And third, Paul established the fact that we are appointed to use the abilities Christ gives in service to Him.

That is The Leadership Life. It is a choice we make, welcoming God into our lives, so that He may express and reveal Himself through us as we live according to the ability He gives. In this way, we honor God and influence others to live life for a higher purpose. Leaders are to live beyond themselves rather than just for themselves. The Leadership Life is living on purpose, with purpose, and for purpose.

We see the same progression of thought from Paul once again in Ephesians 2:10; *For we are His workmanship, created in Christ Jesus for good works, which God prepared beforehand so that we would walk in them.* First, God works in our lives to redeem and renew us through faith in Christ Jesus. Second, this renewal by His Spirit equips and enables us for good works. And third, He has already planned and prepared specific ways for our lives to coincide with His purposes as we carry out these good works.

When we accept this way of life, we receive the capacity to do more than we could do on our own. This capacity for performing good works finds expression by moving its way from our thoughts and eventually into our actions. This is the plan of God, that our personal story of living out the principles of The Leadership Life would glorify Him, benefit others, and bring us fulfillment.

The way I view and understand leadership has been influenced by these principles. For the completion of my graduate studies in organizational leadership I submitted a project paper explaining my personal definition of leadership. I define leadership as:

> *The process of empowering people by directing, nurturing, and activating their capacity for achievement.*

Leadership is an interactive process driven by social influence, which empowers the ability to achieve. This is our experience with how God leads us, and this provides a model for how we lead others.

Jesus told us in John 15:16, *You did not choose me, but I chose you and appointed you so that you might go and bear fruit—fruit that will last—and so that whatever you ask in my name the Father will give you.* Our choice to embrace The Leadership Life is a response to our realization that we have been chosen for a special purpose. God has appointed us to be fruitful and to make a lasting difference in our world. Our leadership perspective becomes a partnership with Him.

The Bible holds many great examples of leadership, men and women who heard the call of God and chose to live The Leadership Life. In this book, I want to take a look at two prominent leadership examples from the Bible. One from the Old Testament and one from the New Testament. The first is the prophet Daniel, who displayed an outstanding attitude of leadership among the challenges of living in a heathen culture. The second is the Apostle Paul, whose unstoppable and incomparable drive to reach the world with the gospel has impacted and inspired leadership thought for many generations.

Their lives provide us with a leadership legacy, and a list of ten significant leadership qualities to emulate. I have been inspired by their outstanding example, and my hope is that this book will become a catalyst for you to gain new insights on effective leadership.

Each chapter contains several key thoughts, which I will highlight for you, as we look at these two men's lives through the lens of leadership. At the end of each chapter is a section for reviewing the leadership concepts, and a section of self-reflective questions. I hope these are helpful to get you thinking about how you can become a better leader. They can also be used for group study or for your own devotional time.

Let's start off with The Leadership Life of Daniel. He was an unusual and intriguing person. I have read through this Old Testament book many times and it always fascinates me.

It holds extraordinary accounts of a man who made a remarkable difference for the work of God in the midst of great difficulties. There are several timeless principles of The Leadership Life for us to discover from this man. Let's begin our journey as we study the meaning of The Leadership Life according to Daniel.

PART 1

THE LEADERSHIP LIFE OF DANIEL

CHAPTER 1

A LIFE OF CONVICTION

But Daniel was determined not to defile himself by eating the food and wine given to them by the king. He asked the chief of staff for permission not to eat these unacceptable foods (Daniel 1:8).

One of the first things we learn about Daniel is that he was a man of conviction. A conviction is a firmly held belief or position, the act or the state of being convinced. It is the demonstrated by taking a stand for what one believes and not compromising those beliefs for any reason. Living a life of strong conviction becomes the foundation for living the Leadership Life.

Chapter one of the book of Daniel reveals that the Babylonian army captured Jerusalem and took the Jewish people into captivity. This occurred because of God's judgment for their prolonged idolatry and rebellion. From among these captives, the king of Babylon sought the brightest and the best youth to be trained as his servants.

This sets the stage for Daniel, a young man forced into a new environment and faced with decisions that challenged his belief system. This is not an easy task for anyone, yet even at his young age, Daniel was resolute in his convictions. He determined in his heart to stay true to the laws of his Jewish faith.

An important part of these laws included specific dietary practices that were meant to reflect absolute devotion to God. To knowingly violate these practices would mean rejecting the heart of his faith. Daniel was offered food and wine from the king's own table, but his mind was already made up. A made up mind can be a powerful asset.

The leadership lesson here is not about dietary habits, although that is a subject worthy of attention. Rather, it speaks to how leadership is built upon dedication to a cause. Leaders live according to principle in the presence of pressure, maintaining their convictions rather than allowing convenience to change them.

That is not to say leaders cannot learn or adopt new ideas. On the contrary, leaders stay fresh and ready by becoming lifelong students and learners. There is much value in seeking wise counsel and being adaptive. Yet, there are fundamental truths and foundational beliefs that must remain non-negotiable. This is what we see taking place in the life of Daniel.

The Leadership Life is built upon a clear purpose. It starts with seeing the big picture and then adhering to the underlying source of personal motivation, which is their guiding values. People achieve great things when they refuse to become swallowed up by the endless demands of daily life and stay mindful of their priorities.

This principle was also evident in the life of Jesus. The gospel accounts record numerous declarations from His own mouth as to why He came. These statements reveal that He possessed an unyielding sense of mission, which sustained Him through to the completion of His assignment from God. If we want to live The Leadership Life, we must do likewise. Let's examine a few of these self-defining statements from the mouth of Jesus.

> Jesus came to serve and give His life - *For even the Son of Man came not to be served but to serve others and to give his life as a ransom for many* (Matthew 28:20).

> Jesus came to seek and save the lost – *For the Son of Man came to seek and to save the lost* (Luke 19:10).

> Jesus came to testify to the truth – *the reason I was born and came into the world is to testify to the truth* (John 18:37).

> Jesus came to do the will of God – *For I have come down from heaven not to do my will but to do the will of him who sent me* (John 6:38).

> Jesus came to be a light - *I have come into the world as a light, so that no one who believes in me should stay in darkness* (John 12:46).

Jesus made several other similar statements, but you get the point. He was keenly self-aware of His life purpose and this understanding generated great personal power. This inner strength keeps us afloat and prevents us from becoming deterred by opposition or obstacles.
Noah didn't back down from building the

ark among the sneers and jeers. Abraham and Sarah clung to the promise of a son when they were well past childbearing age. Moses relentlessly marched his people through difficulties in the wilderness until they were ready to possess their inheritance. Nehemiah led the work to rebuild the walls of Jerusalem in a hostile environment. Paul endured beatings and stoning, shipwrecks and prison, yet he finished his race and kept the faith.

In each of these instances, they overcame substantial challenges and refused to compromise. All these people achieved great things because they shared a common characteristic. They have become examples of faith because they chose to live according to their convictions when confronted with adversity.

The same holds true for anyone else who desires to live the Leadership Life. Your beliefs will be put to the test, questioned and challenged, or perhaps even mocked. Just like Daniel's decision not to partake from the king's table, there will also be crucial moments in your journey that set you apart or hold you back. And just like Daniel, you must decide whether or not to follow your heart or make concessions.

The United States Supreme Court makes an important distinction between what they consider to be a preference as opposed to a conviction. Its ruling is that one's convictions are protected by the Constitution, but not one's preferences. The judges define a preference to be a strong belief, yet one that may be changed under certain circumstances. This differs from holding a conviction, which is seen as an unchangeable belief, something that one believes is required by their God.

We develop strong convictions by making a lifetime commitment to the word of God. It becomes our standard and our authority. It becomes the source of our beliefs and the strength of our soul. The divine power of the Scriptures empowers us to live the Leadership Life.

Most people will tell you they have some set of beliefs, but not everyone actually lives according to what they say they believe. For example, I can say that I believe in God, yet live without any regard to His authority in my life. Some may question whether that proves if I really believe or not, but could the problem be rooted in a lack of commitment to convictions?

Convictions develop when we make a decision to act in accordance with what we believe. The values we hold dear must be translated from ideas into actionable principles. Many people live ineffective lives because they fail to give tangible expression to what they believe. They seem willing to argue for what they believe, but don't seem willing to live and die for what they believe.

Leaders think differently. They take time to think through what matters most and why it matters most. They are more interested in long-term effect than immediate comfort. Their focus on what matters most keeps them from being distracted by anything else, and positions them to achieve.

Personally, I have found meditating on the word of God to be one of the most beneficial practices in my life. It allows me to think deeply about the message of the Scriptures and causes its truth to become imbedded in my soul. This brings the message off the page and into my heart, and helps me to own and personalize it. Now don't let the word "meditation" throw you; that's not assuming a yoga position and humming a mantra, as are often associated with the word meditation. The biblical form of meditation takes place by simply reflecting, rehearsing, and repeating a scripture verse or portion of Scriptures.

For example, I choose a specific Bible verse and think on it, word for word. I take time to walk myself through what it says, and imagine myself acting according to its directive. I declare the verse out loud to myself and ponder on its message as I do. I may even write out the Bible verse on note cards and review it regularly until I have it memorized. But this is more than just memorization, it is a way of assimilating the truth of the message into my life. This process empowers me to act it out.

I spend a lot of time driving, so I made the decision to use that time effectively. When I am on the road, I am usually meditating, praying, or listening to podcasts. This personal commitment to the word of God has made an enormous difference in my life over the years. It refreshes me, inspires me, and encourages me. It helps me to focus on possibilities rather than problems, and keeps me grounded in the faith.

During my college years, I put my faith in Christ for salvation while reading the Bible, and I have been in love with the word of God ever since. Without question, it is the single most influential force in my life. When we decide to make a commitment to the Word of God, we find ourselves ready to act accordingly in the heat of the moment. It prepares and equips us for anything life sends our way. Then when we encounter a situation that challenges us, our response becomes more immediate and instinctive. Rather than having to stop and wrestle with what we should do, the scriptures we have previously meditated on will speak back to us and remind us of what is right.

It all comes back to purpose. Daniel "purposed in his heart" not to be defiled. His firm resolve was founded in his sense of purpose. He was determined to stay loyal to his Jewish roots regardless of his circumstances. He had a clear sense of identity that fortified his decisions, and felt called to uphold specific standards of behavior. This is the basis for a meaningful existence. This is the foundation for the Leadership Life.

Greatness lies within each of us, begging for an opportunity to surface. Our greatness isn't measured only by the size or by the nature of our accomplishments, however, but is also measured by the degree of our commitment to a great cause. The depth of our personal potential becomes equal to the intensity of our devotion. Our greatness is not our own; it is the product of our connection to the greatness of the cause for which we choose to live.

I've heard about certain species of fish that will grow according to their environment. If they are placed in a small aquarium, they will stay small. If they are placed in a pond, they will grow larger. And if they happen to find themselves in the expanse of the ocean, they will respond and grow larger still. We follow a similar pattern.

The Leadership Life transcends our own life. It is always bigger than who we are or what we do. It is an invitation to significance and service. It satisfies the searching soul and grants us the opportunity to participate in something bigger than ourselves. I think of this when I read that Jesus promises us abundant life in John 10:10. Abundant life is a full life; it is a life lived to the fullest measure. To some, living abundantly may sound like the unbridled pursuit of pleasure and self-gratification. To the contrary, abundant life isn't just about having good things; it's also about being a source of blessing to others.

In Romans 15:29, Paul spoke of coming to

Rome in the fullness of the blessing of the gospel of Christ. In Acts 20:35, Jesus told us that it is greater to give than to receive. That tells us the greatest aspect of the gospel isn't only what we can receive from it, but rather what we can offer to others as a result of what we received. Certainly we all must receive from God, but the highest degree of blessing is found in the posture and the desire to serve.

In Acts 26:19, Paul proclaimed that he was not disobedient to the heavenly vision that he had received. Despite encountering many hardships, he refused to back down from his convictions. In 2 Timothy 2:10 he tells us why: *For this reason I endure all things for the sake of God's own people; so that they also may obtain salvation--even the salvation which is in Christ Jesus--and with it eternal glory.* He persevered and endured for the sake of others. His convictions carried him through thick and thin.

Paul was driven by a desire to serve God and to reach people. This is what made him great, and this is what sustained him along the way. While there may be sacrifices associated with living in such a manner, there are also rewards that will elude us otherwise.

The book of Genesis introduces the story of Joseph. As the youngest of twelve brothers, the dreams he spoke about were ridiculed and discounted. His brothers sold him into slavery and he was taken to another country. There, he was falsely accused and ended up in prison. In a place of obscurity and hardship, he didn't lose heart regarding his God-given dreams. Psalm 105:19 tells us, *Until the time that his word came to pass, the word of the Lord tested him.* His deepest convictions were tested by betrayal and injustice, but after many years. his dreams were finally realized. Through a series of amazing events, he suddenly rose to a place of prominence and power, where he served the plan of God to save his nation from famine.

There are many lessons from Joseph's story, but just like Daniel, he displayed a purposed heart that enabled him to overcome adversity. There is a notable difference between the things we *should* do and the things we *must* do. The things we *should* do are good ideas but may not get our full attention. The things we *must* do, however, take us to a whole different level of maturity and wisdom. They leave no question and dissolve any doubt; we have chosen to do these things or die trying.

The Leadership Life is a purposed life.

The Leadership Life is a passionate life.

The Leadership Life is a powerful life.

The Leadership Life is a life lived with conviction.

> **LEADERS LIVE ACCORDING TO PRINCIPLE IN THE PRESENCE OF PRESSURE, MAINTAINING THEIR CONVICTIONS RATHER THAN ALLOWING CONVENIENCE TO CHANGE THEM.**

REVIEW

1. Strong convictions are the foundation for the Leadership Life.

2. Strong convictions are developed through a lifetime commitment to the word of God.

3. Our greatness is found in our connection to a great cause.

4. The Leadership Life is an invitation to significance through service.

5. There is a big difference between the things we feel we *should* do and the things we feel we *must* do.

REFLECTIONS

1. Do you feel as if you have lived life so far by your convictions? Why or why not?

2. Do you agree that a "purposed heart" is the foundation for the Leadership Life? Why or why not?

3. What is the one cause above all others for which you are willing to live and die? How are you currently expressing that in daily life?

CHAPTER 2

A LIFE OF CHARACTER

Daniel then said to the guard whom the chief official had appointed over Daniel, Hananiah, Mishael and Azariah, "Please test your servants for ten days: Give us nothing but vegetables to eat and water to drink. Then compare our appearance with that of the young men who eat the royal food, and treat your servants in accordance with what you see." So he agreed to this and tested them for ten days. At the end of the ten days they looked healthier and better nourished than any of the young men who ate the royal food. So the guard took away their choice food and the wine they were to drink and gave them vegetables instead (Daniel 1:11-16).

As we learned in chapter one, Daniel was a man with strong convictions. He was also a man of great character. If we are to live the Leadership Life designed for us by God, then we must likewise choose a life of honorable character.

All of us have distinctive characteristics that make up our own temperament and personality. In this context, however, character refers to the moral nature and ethical qualities of an individual. It goes beyond merely the personal attributes and traits that distinguish us from others. Our true character is revealed by the virtues and values we personify.

The word integrity usually comes up when we discuss a life of character. Integrity is the quality of moral uprightness, but it also means the state of being whole or undivided. In other words, something or someone that is pure, flawless, or without corruption. An undivided character is completely devoted to one thing with unbreakable loyalty and allegiance. It is proven to be true, accurate, and reliable.

This is exactly what we see taking place in this account of Daniel. First, he purposes in his heart not to be defiled by the foods that violated his conscience, and then he asked to be put to the test. Daniel and his three friends were captives in a foreign land, but they boldly requested a ten day diet of only vegetables and water instead of their portion of the royal food and wine.

At the end of the ten days, Daniel and his friends appeared better than their counterparts, so they were allowed to continue eating their special diet. This story is significant because it reveals several important elements about character. First, it teaches us that our character is developed out of our convictions. Next, it shows that our character is revealed under pressure. Finally, we learn that our character produces credibility.

In the last chapter, we talked about Daniel living a life of conviction, which means he maintained his beliefs no matter the consequence. When we do the same, the development of our character is the result of our commitment to our convictions. If we decide what we believe and hold dear, and then we live inconsistently to those standards, our character is flawed.

For example, when actors revert back to being themselves rather than who they are portraying, it is called breaking character. In fact, actors are applauded and admired for their ability to remain in character despite distractions. In similar fashion, strong moral character is evidenced by someone who is not swayed or moved by external circumstances. They remain true to their embedded values.

Living a life of conviction establishes who we choose to be, what we choose to believe, and how we choose to behave. These kinds of decisions prepare the conditions and the environment in which our character develops. We start out adopting a sense of identity and purpose, and then our subsequent commitment to act in accordance with our values sets the depth of our character.

If we live a disconnected life between our beliefs and our actions, then our leadership potential falls flat. That is precisely why many people have become disenchanted with government and other authority figures. They have witnessed many examples of leaders in name only but not in performance. Poor decisions driven by self-interest have derailed many leaders.

People have come to believe that power corrupts. Yet power is the very thing that Jesus promised to give to His disciples as He returned to heaven. "*I am going to send you what my Fa-*

ther has promised; but stay in the city until you have been clothed with power from on high." (Luke 24:49)

Although people in power have been corrupt, the problem isn't with the power, it's with the people. They have failed to understand or to accept the purpose for the power. "*But you will receive power when the Holy Spirit comes on you; and you will be my witnesses in Jerusalem, and in all Judea and Samaria, and to the ends of the earth*" (Acts 1:8).

When we receive God's power, which is the opportunity and the ability to live the Leadership Life, we must realize the intention of His empowerment. It is intended for service to God and His purposes. To live for anything less than that positions us for a disappointing outcome.

Good character is the result of aligning our daily decisions with our values and dreams. That is why spending time with God in prayer, worship, and meditation is so vital. It maintains a connection with our Creator and nourishes our understanding of who we are and why we are. We receive clarity to keep us on the path of successful living. This ongoing relationship solidifies our knowledge of the image of God we have been granted, and helps prevent a break in character.

Cultivating character establishes healthy boundaries and provides protection. It keeps us in the game with a chance to win. Proverbs 10:9 says, *Whoever walks in integrity walks securely.* If we stay true to who we were meant to be, we stand a better chance of avoiding trouble and fulfilling our full potential.

Consider the way that Satan instigated trouble in the Garden of Eden.

> Now the serpent was more crafty than any of the wild animals the Lord God had made. He said to the

woman, "Did God really say, 'You must not eat from any tree in the garden'?" The woman said to the serpent, "We may eat fruit from the trees in the garden, but God did say, 'You must not eat fruit from the tree that is in the middle of the garden, and you must not touch it, or you will die.' "You will not certainly die," the serpent said to the woman. "For God knows that when you eat from it your eyes will be opened, and you will be like God, knowing good and evil" (Genesis 3:1-5).

Scripture tells us that he tempted them to accept a faulty sense of identity. He told them that eating the forbidden fruit would make them like God, yet they already possessed the image of God and had unrestricted fellowship with Him. They succumbed to temptation because they failed to grasp their identity in God. In their attempt to share God's glory, they disowned their true identity as servants of God and ended up forfeiting their true purpose, which was instead to reflect God's glory.

I've heard it said many times that adversity builds character, but there is something about that perspective that doesn't feel right to me. If that were true, then strong character would be commonplace because all of us encounter some measure of adversity in life. If it was simply a matter of facing hardships and challenges, then the greater degree of adversity would always produce a greater depth of character.

Yet, not all people become better because of what they have been through. The challenges of life do not automatically trigger character development. People of strong character remain difficult to find and highly sought after. That's because it is a matter of our response to the situation that makes the difference.

Evidently, character is not produced by pressure, rather it is revealed under pressure. My dad worked in the steel mill as a metallurgist for many years, testing the quality of steel produced by the plant. Before the parts could be approved for shipment, they would undergo a series of tests to expose cracks or weaknesses in their structure.

In much the same way, the external pressure of the situations we go through merely provide the opportunity for our internal qualities of character to be activated. The resulting behavior then demonstrates the underlying motivation and set of values of the individual.

This is why Daniel could ask to be put to the test. His motives for not eating from the king's table were genuine. He was acting out of his true self. The pressure of the situation revealed him to be a man of high ideals and solid principles. In essence, he was seeking the chance to verify his identity and to clarify his purpose.

This is much like the user name and password on your computer. The operating system asks you to authenticate your identity by providing the correct login credentials. Unless you are authenticated, you will not be granted access. Our character proves who we really are. This produces credibility, which builds trust and preserves our leadership, and authenticates our leadership with others.

At the end of the ten days, Daniel and his friends were proven to be authentic; they were truly who they claimed to be, and they passed the test. In fact, at the end of their three-year period of preparation for service to the king, they were found to be ten times better than all the others (see Daniel 1:20).

I find it significant that they were tested for ten days and then turned out exactly ten times better. Perhaps the lesson is that for each day we choose to authenticate ourselves by staying true to character, we are gaining credibility and strengthening the standard of our leadership.

Leadership is enhanced by trust. Without an ethical framework to order the leader's thoughts and behavior, securing the trust of others is unlikely to happen. Therefore, leadership must include more than only the mechanics of targeted skills and learned behaviors; it must also include a quality of guiding values and principles.

The Scriptures contain several examples that encourage us to consider people for leadership positions based upon attributes of moral character. That is not meant to discount the need for aptitude and ability; certain skill sets can definitely enhance leadership. Yet, in both the Old and New Testaments, the specified qualifications for selecting deacons and other ministry leaders focused on proven lifestyles of ethical practices. Clearly, the potential for successful and enduring leadership is rooted in character.

In Exodus 18, Moses was counseled by his father-in-law, Jethro, to appoint additional leaders to help him with the overwhelming demand of settling cases brought to him by the people. *But select capable men from all the people—men who fear God, trustworthy men who hate dishonest gain—and appoint them as officials over thousands, hundreds, fifties and tens. (Exodus 18:21).* The instruction was not only to find capable men, but also to seek those who displayed respect for God's laws, honesty, and trustworthiness.

In Acts 6, as the early church began to grow, the apostles saw a need to choose helpers to attend to the daily affairs of the church. Once again, the counsel was to seek out men of good moral standing, with both spiritual and natural wisdom. *Therefore, brethren, seek out from among you seven men of good reputation, full of the Holy Spirit and wisdom: whom we may appoint over this business (Acts 6:3).*

Paul wrote to Timothy and Titus about the qualifications he recommended for people to serve as church overseers and leaders. It is interesting to note that Paul primarily listed evidences of good character above anything else.

> *This is a faithful saying: If a man desires the position of a bishop, he desires a good work. A bishop then must be blameless, the husband of one wife, temperate, sober-minded, of good behavior, hospitable, able to teach; not given to wine, not violent, not greedy for money, but gentle, not quarrelsome, not covetous; one who rules his own house well, having his children in submission with all reverence (for if a man does not know how to rule his own house, how will he take care of the church of God?); not a novice, lest being puffed up with pride he fall into the same condemnation as the devil. Moreover he must have a good testimony among those who are outside, lest he fall into reproach and the snare of the devil. Likewise deacons must be reverent, not double-tongued, not given to much wine, not greedy for money, holding the mystery of the faith with a pure conscience. But let these also first be tested; then let them serve as deacons, being found blameless. Likewise, their wives must be reverent,*

not slanderers, temperate, faithful in all things. Let deacons be the husbands of one wife, ruling their children and their own houses well. For those who have served well as deacons obtain for themselves a good standing and great boldness in the faith which is in Christ Jesus (1 Timothy 3:1-13).

An elder must be blameless, faithful to his wife, a man whose children believe and are not open to the charge of being wild and disobedient. Since an overseer manages God's household, he must be blameless—not overbearing, not quick-tempered, not given to drunkenness, not violent, not pursuing dishonest gain. Rather, he must be hospitable, one who loves what is good, who is self-controlled, upright, holy and disciplined. He must hold firmly to the trustworthy message as it has been taught, so that he can encourage others by sound doctrine and refute those who oppose it (Titus 1:6-9).

All too often, people equate leadership ability with external qualities but fail to consider how vital the internal conditions are to leadership. The obvious and the visible usually get more attention than the subtle and the unseen. At the end of the day, however, people of solid character who live by biblical principles stand a much better chance at producing the desired results of an enduring leadership legacy.

The Bible tells us of how King Saul fell from grace and was replaced by King David. The Lord sent Samuel the prophet to anoint one of the sons of Jesse to be the next king. Samuel was impressed by the physical attributes of Jesse's sons, but the Lord quickly reminded him of an important truth: "*But the LORD said to Samuel, "Do not consider his appearance or his height, for I have rejected him. The LORD does not look at the things people look at. People look at the outward appearance, but the LORD looks at the heart" (1 Samuel 16:7).*

David was anointed by Samuel and eventually became one of Israel's greatest kings. He didn't live a perfect life, yet he was regarded by God as "a man after my own heart" (Acts 13:22). David's failures and flaws are openly recorded, yet he was singled out by God as having a unique leadership quality - he had integrity of heart:

> *He chose David his servant and took him from the sheep pens; from tending the sheep he brought him to be the shepherd of his people Jacob, of Israel his inheritance. And David shepherded them with integrity of heart; with skillful hands he led them (Psalm 78:70-72).*

Having integrity of heart didn't mean that David wasn't prone to mistakes. It means that David was prone to self-examination and correction:

> *Search me, God, and know my heart; test me and know my anxious thoughts. See if there is any offensive way in me, and lead me in the way everlasting (Psalm 139:23-24).*

Just like David, we need to search our hearts with God's help so we can make adjustments as we travel along the journey of life. It can be a fearful thing to behold what is truly in our hearts, but more importantly it can prove to be one of the most liberating things we will ever do. We can't be ourselves if we are not willing to be honest with ourselves. As we walk with God, He can help us exchange the false for what is true, and the fleeting for what is enduring.

I have made it my prayer for years that God would help me love what He loves, to hate what He hates, and to help me want what He wants for the same reasons He wants it. This is part of becoming who He intends for me to be. Part of being a leader is helping others to envision and to embrace what they are capable of.

We can't take others to places where we haven't already been. Leading with integrity means becoming transparent with yourself. Allow God to reveal His vision for you and be willing to make the journey. Only then can you make peace with God and with yourself. Only then can you assume your appropriate character, the one you were made for. Only then can we inspire others to do likewise.

The Leadership Life is a principled life.

The Leadership Life is an authentic life.

The Leadership Life is a relevant life.

The Leadership Life is a life built on character.

> **LIVING A LIFE OF CONVICTION ESTABLISHES WHO WE CHOOSE TO BE, WHAT WE CHOOSE TO BELIEVE, AND HOW WE CHOOSE TO BEHAVE.**

REVIEW

1. Our character develops from living out our convictions.
2. Our character is revealed under pressure.
3. Our leadership credibility is proportional to our character.
4. Our character verifies our true identity and clarifies our true purpose.
5. Our potential for authentic and enduring leadership is rooted in character.

REFLECTIONS

1. What are the primary values that uphold your character?
2. Do you agree that one's potential for leadership is rooted in character? Why or why not?
3. What are you already doing, or what could you begin doing, that would strengthen your character?

CHAPTER 3

A LIFE OF COMPETENCE

Now Daniel so distinguished himself
among the administrators and the
satraps by his exceptional qualities
that the king planned to set him
over the whole kingdom
(Daniel 6:3).

Daniel exhibited outstanding leadership through a life of conviction, a life of character, and also through a life of competence. The biblical record states that Daniel was distinguished among his peers because of his exceptional qualities. He proved himself uncommonly capable and without equal. Daniel was in a class all by himself. Daniel had a spirit of excellence.

Maybe you're thinking that I am contradicting myself after spending the last chapter explaining why matters of character take precedence over matters of ability, but this is not an either-or proposition. I am not saying we need to sacrifice ability for the sake of character. It's

25

more a matter of sequence and progression. Convictions shape character and then character sets the stage for competency to flex its muscles. Weak character dooms leadership by failing to provide safe boundaries that lead to good behavior.

To the contrary, strong character establishes a healthy atmosphere for potential to flourish. Someone with much ability but little character can achieve a certain level of success, but eventually their character deficiencies will limit their effectiveness. It is best to begin by building a foundation of conviction and character upon which your abilities can emerge and be maximized.

Perhaps you don't consider yourself as a leader or don't currently hold a formal leadership position. Keep in mind that's not all there is to leadership. Let me reiterate that each of us is called to exercise leadership in a particular area of gifting and talent. Sometimes those abilities come so naturally that we take them for granted and fail to realize it is part of God's design for our lives.

Proverbs 18:16 tells us, *A man's gift makes room for him, and brings him before great men.* There is an individual giftedness that each of us is entrusted with from our Creator. People often equate this with obvious examples such as entertainers or athletes. As leaders, there are however, many other qualities that may not be as noticeable, yet should not be regarded as less important. You possess some ability that has been specifically granted for the purposes of furthering God's kingdom and serving your fellow man. Your gift making room for you means that your exceptional competence in a certain area will create an opportunity for you. What you do with that opportunity is part of how God will judge your life someday.

In Genesis 1, the Bible reveals that God created mankind to rule the earth as His stewards. This truth is found again in Psalm 8, when David declared that God put mankind in charge of everything He made. Each of us was created with an innate sense of authority, and an instinctive desire to govern our surroundings. This awareness has been dulled or perverted at times, causing some people to suppress and take advantage of others, but the original intent is clear. God created people to share the responsibility of ruling His world, and He strategically equips each of us to carry out our assigned areas of responsibility in unique ways.

Jesus told the parable of the talents in Matthew 25. Three servants were entrusted by their master with different amounts of money, or we could say different measures of ability. When the master returned home after a long trip, he asked for a report of their activities while he was away. Likewise, we are accountable to the Lord for what He has given to us. In Luke's account of the same parable, the servants are instructed to put the money to work (see Luke 19:13). Two of the servants did just that and upon the master's return, they were congratulated and rewarded, while the other servant was severely reprimanded for his lack of foresight and effort.

In practical terms, this parable teaches us that our responsibility is to discover our purpose, develop our potential, and do our part in the work of God's kingdom. We don't need to be the president, a CEO, or some other version of an executive to be a leader. I'm not saying we shouldn't aim high or think big, I'm simply saying the Leadership Life is for everyone. Each of the servants in the parable Jesus told received something. Paul compared the church to a body in which each part functions as it was intended (see Ephesians 4:16). Likewise, each of us was born with something of value, the ability to exert extraordinary competence in some area.

Competence isn't about achieving average or ordinary results, it refers to setting the standard for specific skills and behaviors that contribute to excellence. Competence displays a pattern or an example of how something should be done. The Leadership Life begins when we understand we were born with something to give, and we decide to make it happen as often as possible.

Don't get caught up in comparing yourself to others or wishing for someone else's life. This seems to be the approach of most advertising campaigns and often gives way to negative and counterproductive emotions such as pride, jealousy, or apathy. Rather than devaluing what you have to offer, become aware of your unique qualities and then pursue excellence by demanding the best from yourself.

A spirit of excellence isn't bestowed from above to only a select few. It is achieved by those who seek to excel in their abilities. While it is true that not all people have been granted equal ability, we each still have an equal opportunity to achieve excellence. That is because excellence is not only the result of what we have been given, but also by what we do with what we have been given. Our success can be defined by reaching the full potential of our abilities.

Aristotle said that we are what we repeatedly do. Therefore, excellence is not an isolated act but a habit. We are looking to establish patterns of principles and practices that produce proficiency. Our primary goal, however, should be more than what we do, it should be who we are, because who we are determines what we do.

I associate excellence with reaching our full potential. Since each of us has some level of potential or natural ability, then each of us has some way to achieve excellence. The starting point of excellence is discerning our giftedness, but it can only reach full maturity through faith and action. It is not only doing the right thing or doing things the right way, it is a combination of doing the right things in the right way over and over again. We achieve an excellent spirit by developing a habit of pursuing and cultivating the exceptional abilities that God has placed within us.

This is how Daniel gained such a powerful reputation in Babylon. He put his abilities to work and soon became known for those exceptional qualities. He was recognized as a leader through his regular displays of competence and excellence. When we are where God wants us to be, doing what God wants us to do, and doing it with the proper attitude, the greatness that lies within us begins to emerge:

> *There is a man in your kingdom in whom is the spirit of the holy gods...This was because an extraordinary spirit, knowledge and insight, interpretation of dreams, explanation of enigmas, and solving difficult problems were found in this Daniel (Daniel 5:11-12).*

Daniel was recognized for his outstanding attitude and approach to solving problems. His perspective and manner for bringing understanding and direction in the midst of confusion were quickly noticed. He became the go-to guy whenever answers were needed. That is precisely the role the church should be playing in the world today. We should be the ones the world turns to for answers and instruction. We should be the ones known for cutting through the fog and giving direction.

Daniel was valued because of a spirit of excellence. A spirit of excellence gets people's attention, creates confidence, and gathers an audience. Living a life of competence is more than just getting the job done, it sets the standard for how it should be done. Proverbs 22:29 tells us, *Do you see any truly competent workers? They will serve kings rather than working for ordinary people.* In this context, competence is depicted as being worthy of serving the highest office in the land. It is associated with doing work of the utmost importance. It is regarded as a quality desired by kings and rulers. Competence opens the door to living a life of influence.

True competence goes beyond the ordinary or the mediocre. A commitment to excellence becomes the signature of the Leadership Life. Yet it's not about achieving perfection or proving our superiority over others. It's more than getting a name for ourselves or finding a place in the record books. It's really about giving glory to God, who is the model of excellence.

Our attitude and motivation factor into bringing glory to God. We do well when our pursuit of excellence flows from gratitude for our abilities, and comes with the intent of honoring God as the source of our achievements.

> *You are the light of the world. A town built on a hill cannot be hidden. Neither do people light a lamp and put it under a bowl. Instead they put it on its stand, and it gives light to everyone in the house. In the same way, let your light shine before others, that they may see your good deeds and glorify your Father in heaven (Matthew 5:14-16).*

The light is meant to be seen and the results of our leadership are intended to be noticed. Yet, it is the unseen motive of our heart that produces a genuine spirit of excellence. When we view the development of our competence as accepting God's invitation to participate in His excellence, it then becomes an act of worship. Let us choose to humbly embrace our capabilities as the gift of God, and then endeavor to give those qualities full expression for His service.

The Apostle Paul instructs us in Colossians 3:23, *Whatever you do, work at it with all your heart, as though you were working for the Lord and not for people.* In Romans 1:15 Paul wrote, *So, as much as is in me, I am ready to preach the gospel to you who are in Rome also.* He clearly served the Lord wholeheartedly and was committed to living for the glory of God.

Again, we can see his commitment to excellence displayed in his letter to the Corinthian church. *Don't you realize that in a race everyone runs, but only one person gets the prize? So run to win! (1 Corinthians 9:24).*

The admonition of running to win encourages us to seek our personal best in the race of life. It is a reminder to stay focused on what matters most, living a disciplined life that serves God. Each of us has a course to follow and a race to run. Yet the Christian life is not designed as a competition against each other. God is a rewarder of those who seek Him (Hebrews 11:6) but let's not reduce our call to simply a desire for personal gain. On the other hand, we should not be satisfied with merely giving a nominal or a mediocre effort. There is too much at stake for us to do that.

Just like Paul, let's have a run-to-win mindset. Let's join the race and never look back. Let's choose to follow Solomon's instruction, "*What-*

31

ever your hand finds to do, do it with all your might"…. (Ecclesiastes 9:10).

Just like Daniel, let's be remarkable and stand out among the crowd and be known for an excellent spirit. Let's trust in God who gives the ability, and then let's apply ourselves whole-heartedly to be the vessel through which those abilities can produce extraordinary results:

> *Therefore, my dear brothers and sisters, stand firm. Let nothing move you. Always give yourselves fully to the work of the Lord, because you know that your labor in the Lord is not in vain (1 Corinthians 15:58).*

The Leadership Life is an excellent life.

The Leadership Life is a committed life.

The Leadership Life is an exceptional life.

The Leadership Life is a life lived with competence.

> **EACH OF US WAS CREATED WITH AN INNATE SENSE OF AUTHORITY, AND AN INSTINCTIVE DESIRE TO GOVERN OUR SURROUNDINGS.**

REVIEW

1. Good character sets the stage for competency to perform.
2. Each of us is called to exercise leadership in a particular area of gifting and ability.
3. Our God-given ability reveals our area of responsibility.
4. A spirit of excellence comes from demanding the best from ourselves and seeking our full potential.
5. Excellence is more of a habit than an event.

REFLECTIONS

1. How do you define a spirit of excellence?
2. Do you agree that a spirit of excellence is an attitude of worship? Why or why not?
3. What personal habits and disciplines are you working on to increase your leadership competency?

CHAPTER 4

A LIFE OF CONSISTENCY

> *So the governors and satraps sought to find some charge against Daniel concerning the kingdom; but they could find no charge or fault, because he was faithful; nor was there any error or fault found in him. Then these men said, "We shall not find any charge against this Daniel unless we find it against him concerning the law of his God"*
> *(Daniel 6:4-5).*

In the last chapter, we discussed how Daniel was distinguished among his peers. He was esteemed as a leader because of his exceptional qualities. As he discerned his unique ability to add value to others, and as he committed himself to the development of those abilities, he became recognized for having a spirit of excellence.

As we continue with the story of Daniel, we learn about another remarkable attribute of his.

Daniel proved himself to be faithful. One of the things that set him apart was his constant trustworthiness. His spirit of excellence was linked to his faithfulness. In other words, Daniel lived a life of consistency.

Faithfulness can be defined in several ways, but I like to think of it as simply exercising our faith. Just as regular exercise builds our muscle tone, consistently applying our faith makes our faith stronger and more enduring. We don't achieve physical fitness with just one workout, and neither will we become faithful with just one decision to follow the Lord. Faithfulness is making continual choices to follow Him.

Being faithful means being full of faith. Real faith always leads to corresponding action. Therefore, we could say that faithfulness is found in the consistent application of fundamental beliefs and principles. For me, the key word in all of this is consistency.

The idea of consistency may appear boring or dull to some. It's not a glamorous term, nor does it give the impression of being exciting or stimulating. Yet when it comes to the Leadership Life, consistency is an essential ingredient.

Consistency is the result of discipline, and discipline is directed by our value system. Our values are the result of our beliefs. This progression of thought brings me to the conclusion that leadership effectiveness is directly related to consistent upright behavior. What we believe, we will eventually value. What we value, we will eventually pursue. Ultimately, our pursuit is characterized by consistent behavior.

Why is this important? It is important because establishing consistent behavior sets in motion the opportunity for accountability. Achieving accountability then generates predictability. Strong predictability gives support to credibility, and leadership cannot exist without credibility. Leadership influence requires trust, and trust is difficult to build without exhibiting consistent behavior.

Consistency in thought and action displays faithfulness to principles and standards. This encourages confidence from others and invites cooperation. Anything less breeds confusion and disunity, which weakens leadership.

In the story of Daniel, those opposed to him plotted his demise based upon his predictability. They scrutinized his life, but they couldn't find fault with him because he was faithful. His excellence emerged from behaviors that he repeated. He stayed true to his conscience and acted accordingly. Faithful people are focused people who don't make room for distraction.

Amazingly, Daniel's enemies felt they had no other choice but to develop a scheme against him that actually counted on his faithfulness. They knew he prayed to the Lord three times a day, so they enacted a law that made it illegal to pray to anyone except the king for thirty days. They fully expected Daniel to continue praying to God as he always did. True to form, Daniel did exactly as they anticipated. Their scheme eventually imploded upon them; they were thrown to the lions and Daniel was set free. We see from this story that faithful people rise above the challenges of life.

Think of faithfulness as a default setting. Many types of equipment are manufactured with factory defaults that can be activated to resolve malfunctions. In much the same way, we can build recurring habits into our lives to serve as automatic responses that keep us from malfunctioning.

The power of habit and how it can impact our lives are fascinating studies. We tend to think of habits in a negative context, yet that is not the complete picture. Rather, I encourage you to consider the positive value contained in a habit and how consistency in action fosters personal effectiveness.

I have personally experienced how this can work. Around the age of twelve, I developed an interest in lifting weights. It is something I have enjoyed ever since. Over the years, I have come to realize that in addition to the physical benefits, the consistent discipline of fitness training can be helpful in other ways as well.

There is an amount of mental toughness that comes by showing up at the gym day after day and completing the workout. With each repetition of each set, there is a decision to see it through to the end. By pushing and pulling through the physical discomfort, my mind gets trained, too. My mind gets less accustomed to backing down from challenges, and becomes more intent on reaching the goal.

The unexpected benefit is that the discipline of physical training carries over into other areas of life. The more I stand up to the demands of the training, the more confident my thinking becomes in the face of other challenges. Developing the habit of moving past perceived limits activates an internal drive to continue going forward. The result is consistent behavior that fosters discipline and generates focus. Ultimately, a disciplined mind positively influences personal effectiveness.

The Leadership Life is living with awareness that we are entrusted by God with gifts and abilities to be used in His service (see 1 Timothy 1:12). Consistent behavior means becoming disciplined in ways that enhance the potential of those abilities. It is an act of consecration and dedication to God's plan. Our faithfulness is necessary for leadership success.

I'm not talking about becoming a robot or a zombie; I am talking about the power faithfulness has to build credibility and confidence. One of the primary attributes of God is His faithfulness. There are dozens of Bible verses about God's great faithfulness, and here are just a few.

- Hebrews 13:8 tells us that, *Jesus Christ is the same yesterday and today and forever.*

- Malachi 3:6 reads, *I the Lord do not change*.

- Lamentations 3:22-23 reminds us: *The steadfast love of the Lord never ceases; His mercies never come to an end; they are new every morning; great is your faithfulness*.

- *Psalms 86:15 states, "But you, O Lord, are a God merciful and gracious, slow to anger and abounding in steadfast love and faithfulness."*

- *Deuteronomy 7:9 says, Know therefore that the LORD your God is God, the faithful God who keeps covenant and steadfast love with those who love him and keep his commandments, to a thousand generations...*

- *Psalms 89:8 O Lord God of hosts, who is mighty as you are, O Lord, with your faithfulness all around you?*

- *Hebrews 10:23 reminds us, Let us hold fast the confession of our hope without wavering, for he who promised is faithful.*

God's faithfulness is a source of strength for us in a world filled with uncertainty. Life brings risks and challenges, but living by faith empowers us to overcome them all. Some may think that mindset is blind or misguided, but living by faith is simply trusting in God's faithfulness. Our faith is to be modeled after His faithfulness. Like Abraham and his wife Sarah, we get good results when we consider God to be faithful to His promises (see Hebrews 11:11).

Hebrews chapter six outlines more details on how God assured Abraham and Sarah of the certainty of His promise.

> *When God made his promise to Abraham, since there was no one greater for him to swear by, he swore by himself, saying, "I will surely bless you and give you many descendants."And so after waiting patiently, Abraham received what was promised. People swear by someone greater than themselves, and the oath confirms what is said and puts an end to all argument. Because God wanted to make the unchanging nature of his purpose very clear to the heirs of what was promised, he confirmed it with an oath. God did this so that, by two unchangeable things in which it is impossible for God to lie, we who have fled to take hold of the hope set before us may be greatly encouraged... (Hebrews 6:13-18).*

When God made His promise to Abraham, He confirmed it with two unchangeable things. The first was with the fact that God cannot lie; He is truth and it is not in His nature to be otherwise. The second is that He made an oath, which simply means that He placed Himself under penalty if He did not make good on His promise. That means God is so committed to being faithful, that He is willing to surrender His throne if He breaks His promise. When we realize the magnitude of His commitment to faithfulness, it brings us great encouragement to trust Him and to follow His lead.

If God puts such a high premium on being faithful, it stands to reason that He also expects faithfulness from His people. Paul explained, *This, then, is how you ought to regard us: as servants of Christ and as those entrusted with the mysteries God has revealed. Now it is required that those who have been given a trust must prove faithful. (1 Corinthians 4:1-2)*

If we intend to live the Leadership Life, we must commit to faithfulness. When we do that, our consistency instills trust in others and encourages them to follow our lead. The world is desperate for faithful people. One of the primary reasons people give for not accepting the message of the church is the hypocrisy of Christians. Inconsistency and unfaithfulness are distasteful even to unbelievers. In the end, they will still be accountable to God for their decision to reject the gospel, but the truth remains that faithfulness gets people's attention and endorses what we stand for.

According to the psalmist, we can learn the ways of the Lord, and begin to focus on faithfulness. As we learn from the Lord to rely on His faithfulness, it leads to living with an undivided heart. *"Teach me your way, Lord, that I may rely on your faithfulness; give me an undivided heart, that I may fear your name" (Psalm 86:11).*

Living with an undivided heart produces a single-minded devotion and relentless consistency. An undivided heart is not easily distracted, nor easily moved off task. An undivided heart is not scattered, nor indifferent, but approaches life with clear priorities and boundless energy.

41

An undivided heart is strong and steadfast, purposed and self-aware. These are the makings of a lifestyle of faithfulness.

Many claim to have unfailing love, but a faithful person *who can find? (Proverbs 20:6).*

Some things never change, as we can see from the writer of the book of Proverbs. Even then, it wasn't easy to find someone whose actions matched their words. Faithfulness and dependability will remain characteristics that set people apart from the norm. May God help us to be the faithful people the world is looking for. May we live a life of integrity and truth that inspires confidence in others to embrace our message. May we become known for our faithfulness as Daniel was.

The commitment to faithfulness comes with a price. It will require a measure of sacrifice and difficult decisions. It may stretch you beyond your comfort zones. But keep in mind the promise of Proverbs 28:20, *A faithful man will abound with blessings.*

The Leadership Life is a disciplined life.

The Leadership Life is a faithful life.

The Leadership Life is a consecrated life.

The Leadership Life is a life of consistency.

> **FAITHFULNESS IS FOUND IN THE CONSISTENT APPLICATION OF FUNDAMENTAL BELIEFS AND PRINCIPLES.**

Review

1. Consistency is a vital part of a commitment to excellence.
2. Faithfulness can be defined as consistently exercising our faith.
3. Consistency in leadership generates a healthy predictability and accountability.
4. Faithfulness is found in dedication and consecration to God's plan.
5. Focusing on God's faithfulness produces an undivided heart within us.

Reflections

1. How do you define faithfulness?
2. Do you agree that consistency is the result of discipline? Why or why not?
3. How might you become more consistent in your leadership?

CHAPTER 5

A LIFE OF COMPASSION

"And now, O Lord our God, who have brought Your people out of the land of Egypt with a mighty hand and have made a name for Yourself, as it is this day—we have sinned, we have been wicked. O Lord, in accordance with all Your righteous acts, let now Your anger and Your wrath turn away from Your city Jerusalem, Your holy mountain; for because of our sins and the iniquities of our fathers, Jerusalem and Your people have become a reproach to all those around us. So now, our God, listen to the prayer of Your servant and to his supplications, and for Your sake, O Lord, let Your face shine on Your desolate sanctuary. O my God, incline Your ear and hear! Open Your eyes and see our

45

> *desolations and the city which
> is called by Your name; for we are
> not presenting our supplications
> before You on account of any merits
> of our own, but on account of Your
> great compassion. O Lord, hear!
> O Lord, forgive! O Lord, listen and
> take action! For Your own sake,
> O my God, do not delay, because
> Your city and Your people are called
> by Your name" (Daniel 9:15-19).*

Without a doubt, Daniel was a great man who lived a highly influential life. In this final chapter about him, I want to focus on another important leadership indicator that is the crowning aspect of Daniel's life. We've already discussed how Daniel left his mark through a lifestyle of conviction, character, competency, and consistency. I want to add another element to that distinguished list. Daniel summed up the essence of The Leadership Life by exhibiting a life of compassion.

In Daniel chapter nine, we gain insight into his prayer life, which grants us insight into his heart, and reveals what truly motivated him. Daniel understood, by reading the writings of Jeremiah, that Israel would be captive in Babylon for seventy years. He was moved to intercede by confessing the sins of the nation and seeking restoration by God's intervention. As one of the most powerful men in the Babylonian government, he had achieved a level of personal comfort, yet he was sensitive to the realities of human need outside the context of his life of privilege.

Clearly, he was zealous for the good of his people and for the name of his God. He was empathetic to the collective need of his generation, and was intent on supporting the greater good.

His prayers give evidence that he lived life with a heart of compassion.

This compassionate approach to life epitomized his spirit of excellence. Compassion can be explained as a genuine concern for others, followed by the will to act on their behalf. It is comprised of three caring characteristics: empathy, affection, and motivation. The starting point is taking notice of another's situation and emotionally sharing in his or her experience. From this understanding, an approach of benevolent and meaningful action begins to form.

The original meaning of the word compassion includes "suffering together with" and actually indicates the bowels or intestines of a person. In other words, compassion is feeling for someone else's need from the innermost and deepest part of one's being. This is not the lifestyle of the selfish and heartless. Selfishness comes easily, but the decision to live a life of compassionate service "requires guts."

Compassion is greatness is action. It reveals the depth of one's soul, and becomes the platform for one's legacy. In the end, what we do on behalf of others will count infinitely more in God's sight than what we do for ourselves. A life of compassion goes beyond empathizing with the plight of people, it actually places the finger of our understanding upon the pulse of God. We begin to feel His heartbeat for serving and to sense His passion for bringing people to wholeness.

The heart of God is revealed in John 3:16: *For this is how God loved the world: He gave his one and only Son, so that everyone who believes in him will not perish but have eternal life.* He did more than just sympathize with the fact that we were lost in sin; He took action at enormous personal cost to correct the situation. He is the epitome of selfless compassion.

When Jesus walked the earth, He was moved with compassion by the suffering of humanity: *When he saw the crowds, he had compassion on them because they were confused and helpless, like sheep without a shepherd (Matthew 9:36).*

It is important to note Jesus' response to this situation of humanity. When confronted with the burdens of the people, He felt compassion but He didn't just stop there. He called for loving action as we can see from the next two verses: *He said to his disciples, "The harvest is great, but the workers are few. So pray to the Lord who is in charge of the harvest; ask him to send more workers into his fields" (Matthew 9:37-38).*

In essence, He was telling all of us that we can and should do something about people in need. It starts with paying attention and spending time with people so that we become aware of their needs. From there, we can assume responsibility for their needs by praying for them. Our prayers release the power of God to bring about change in the world. The change comes in the form of a willing heart that goes to work in the harvest fields. None of us can do everything for everybody, but each of us can pray, joining our hearts with God to become vessels for His work in a needy world.

Jesus' great heart of compassion caused Him to reach out with a healing hand: *Jesus saw the huge crowd as he stepped from the boat, and he had compassion on them and healed their sick (Matthew 14:14).* The healing power of God is available to repair, restore, and renew the broken parts of people's lives. That kind of power is activated when we respond with compassion.

Jesus wept over the city of Jerusalem as He reflected on how eagerly He desired to rescue them: *When He approached Jerusalem,* He saw the city and wept over it, *saying, If you had known in this day, even you, the things which make for peace! But now they have been hidden from your eyes (Luke 19:41-42).*

Matthew records another instance of Jesus expressing His willingness to help, when He said, *O Jerusalem, Jerusalem, the city that kills the prophets and stones God's messengers! How often I have wanted to gather your children together as a hen protects her chicks beneath her wings, but you wouldn't let me (Matthew 23:37).*

Often such an attitude seems incongruent with leadership. Some people misunderstand humility and compassion on the part of leadership as being soft and weak. In reality, studies show the opposite effect. Again and again, research proves that compassionate leadership breeds a positive and productive organizational culture.

Jim Collins, the highly respected and best-selling author of business blockbusters like *Good to Great* and *Built to Last*, describes this as Level Five leadership. His research explains that the best performing organizations are usually led by those with great ambition mixed with great humility. Level Five leaders may seem quiet and unassuming, yet they are driven by a desire for the greater good. The gentle outward persona belies the inward inferno of altruistic energy. These types of leaders have mastered the ability to perceive the real need, and to effectively respond by determining the best course of action.

Compassionate leadership is less about command and control, and more about connect and care. It is less about telling people what to do, and more about building genuine relationships. Such leaders possess a peripheral vision that allows them to see the big picture. They notice others and what they are up against. Then with a selfless and benevolent spirit, they take ownership of the situation. Leading from this perspective of personal responsibility and connectivity causes others to mobilize their efforts and achieve extraordinary results.

Leading with compassion engenders a spirit of service and empowerment in followers. We offer our service as a gift to others because we have first received it ourselves: *We love Him because He first loved us (1 John 4:19).* This gift we give becomes a seed that bears fruit in others. It is leading by example, and generates a productive atmosphere of hope and positive energy.

Our contemporary culture is steeped in consumerism, and unfortunately that attitude has also permeated the church. It takes a conscious and intentional decision to resist the pull of the world toward the attitude "what's in it for me?" Most people would agree that something needs to be done to address the myriad of problems in the world, yet finding people willing to give of themselves is less common.

Perhaps that is because their attention has been misdirected. Rather than asking "what's in it for me?", maybe a better question is "what's been done for me?" When we realize the vast exchange that was made on our behalf by Christ, we cannot help but experience transformation. Paul wrote in Romans 12:1-2,

> *Therefore, I urge you, brothers and sisters, in view of God's mercy, to offer your bodies as a living sacrifice, holy and pleasing to God—this is your true and proper worship. Do not conform to the pattern of this world, but be transformed by the renewing of your mind. Then you will be able to test and approve what God's will is—his good,*

pleasing and perfect will.

In view of God's great mercy toward us, it is reasonable and proper to offer ourselves to Him in worship and in service. Our approach and our attitude about life become transformed when we realize how gracious He has been to each of us. We miss opportunities to make a difference when we focus on the cost of serving, rather than on the wealth of what we have received. Such a narrow focus keeps our goals too small and our reach too short. When we receive the gift of Christ's redemption, not only do we exchange our sin for His salvation, but we also exchange our small thinking for His big vision. Not only are we saved from the penalty of sin, but we are rescued from an aimless and meaningless fate. We enter into His purpose and we become an extension of His love.

Daniel lived through the Babylonian exile of the Jewish people. He identified himself with their hurt and loss. He declared that "*we have sinned*" as he sought God's merciful restoration. Likewise, Jesus lived among us as a man, became acquainted with the human condition, and felt the weight of our need. As our leader, He understands and responds with mercy and grace:

> *So then, since we have a great High Priest who has entered heaven, Jesus the Son of God, let us hold firmly to what we believe. This High Priest of ours understands our weaknesses, for he faced all of the same testings we do, yet he did not sin. So let us come boldly to the throne of our gracious God. There we will receive his mercy, and we will find grace to help us when we need it most (Hebrews 4:14-16).*

In Luke 10, Jesus told the parable of the

Good Samaritan. This man stopped along the road to help another who was left for dead by bandits. Two other travelers preceded the Good Samaritan but did not stop to help the injured man. Jesus contrasted these two responses and encouraged us to follow the Good Samaritan's leadership example:

> *"Now which of these three would you say was a neighbor to the man who was attacked by bandits?" Jesus asked. The man replied, "The one who showed him mercy." Then Jesus said, "Yes, now go and do the same" (Luke 10:36-37).*

To go and do the same, as Jesus instructs us, requires compassionate leadership. This quality is produced through a process of personal transformation, resulting in humble hearts that are grateful for the opportunity to give back. Authentic leadership is found in those, like Daniel, who have come to terms with their call to relate and to respond to the needs around them. Leaders see what others don't, and leaders care when others won't.

Pride can be subtle, but it always deceives. By masking the truth, pride prevents us from stepping into the fullness of God's plan for our lives. Pride makes us forgetful of God's grace and keeps us isolated on a path of ineffective and small living. First Peter 5:5 reminds us that, *God resists the proud but gives grace to the humble.* His grace frees us to engage the needs of others, and enlarges our heart toward them.

Compassion is energized by gaining a new perspective for people – Christ's perspective. When we understand that only by God's grace is our life experience any different from theirs, it activates and adjusts our sense of purpose. Every need that we encounter speaks the language of God. It is His invitation to participate in the ongoing work of redemption and renewal. It is His call to The Leadership Life.

The Leadership Life is a motivated life.

The Leadership Life is a generous life.

The Leadership Life is an engaged life.

The Leadership Life is a life driven by compassion.

COMPASSION IS FEELING FOR SOMEONE ELSE'S NEED FROM THE INNERMOST AND DEEPEST PART OF ONE'S BEING.

REVIEW

1. Compassion is a genuine concern for others followed by the will to act on their behalf.
2. Compassion is a process of empathy, affection, and motivation to act on the behalf of others.
3. Compassion is greatness in action.
4. Compassionate leadership breeds a positive and productive organizational culture.
5. Compassionate leadership emanates from those with great ambition coupled with great humility.

REFLECTIONS

1. Do you agree that compassion is an important aspect of leadership? Why or why not?
2. How have you tried to lead with compassion? Has it produced good results?
3. How can you begin to cultivate a more compassionate leadership style?

PART 2

THE LEADERSHIP LIFE OF PAUL

CHAPTER 6

A TRANSFORMED LIFE

The life of the Apostle Paul fills much of the New Testament, and it is a remarkable story. His lifestyle is exemplary and his contribution to history and the church are unparalleled. He was and remains, a true champion of the cause of Jesus Christ.

When we read about his many exploits, we see how his influence helped to advance the gospel to the known world in his own lifetime. We read his letters to the churches that outline many fundamental doctrines of the faith. We see the mighty results of his apostleship and his travels. As important as those things are, it motivates me to look into how he became such a stalwart leader. What actually went into the making of a man like this? What catalyzed his leadership life?

Paul mentions something quite interesting in Galatians 6:17. Throughout the letter he explained that some are challenging his leadership and questioning his authority. Just as Moses, David, and even Jesus, encountered resistance to

57

their leadership, the opposition was demanding validation from the Apostle Paul. He concluded his letter to the church with this statement: *From now on let no one trouble me, for I bear in my body the marks of the Lord Jesus.* There are many varying interpretations of the meaning of this, but I want to bring out one primary thought.

Leadership is a "contact sport", and choosing to live the Leadership Life leaves a mark. Just like any journey, there are noteworthy landmarks to be seen along the way. Whether Paul was referencing physical scars or perhaps another type of imprint upon his life, the point is that there are hallmark moments in The Leadership Life that we can identify and learn from. There are outward evidences of the inner life of any leader that are significant to our study. Just as we did for Daniel, I want us to examine several leadership landmarks from the life of the Apostle Paul.

In Acts chapter 26, Paul finds himself in a familiar position when he was on trial, giving a defense of his faith. From his own mouth, we discover several details of his early experience that were foundational to his development as a leader. In verses 12 through 23, Paul explains to King Agrippa how he was converted to Christ and how he lived from that day forward. Against this backdrop, we are given a glimpse into The Leadership Life of Paul:

> " *While thus occupied, as I journeyed to Damascus with authority and commission from the chief priests, at midday, O king, along the road I saw a light from heaven, brighter than the sun, shining around me and those who journeyed with me. And when we all had fallen to the ground, I heard*

a voice speaking to me, and saying in the Hebrew language, Saul, Saul, why are you persecuting Me? It is hard for you to kick against the goads. So I said, Who art You, Lord? And He said, I am Jesus, whom you are persecuting. But rise and stand on your feet: for I have appeared to you for this purpose, to make you a minister and a witness both of the things which you have seen and of the things which I will yet reveal to you. I will deliver you from the Jewish people, as well as from the Gentiles, to whom I now send you, to open their eyes, in order to turn them from darkness to light, and from the power of Satan to God, that they may receive forgiveness of sins, and an inheritance among those who are sanctified by faith in Me. Therefore, King Agrippa, I was not disobedient to the heavenly vision: but declared first to those in Damascus and in Jerusalem, and throughout all the region of Judea, and then to the Gentiles, that they should repent, turn to God, and do works befitting repentance. For these reasons the Jews seized me in the temple and tried to kill me. Therefore, having obtained help from God, to this day I stand, witnessing both to small and great, saying no other things than those which the prophets and Moses said would come: that the Christ would suffer, that He would be the first to rise from the dead, and would proclaim light to the Jewish people, and to the Gentiles."

Something with immense consequences happened to Saul of Tarsus on the way to Damascus. He traveled from Jerusalem to Damascus with a mindset that was vehemently opposed to Christianity, and he returned as its most ardent spokesperson. He set out emboldened with a commission and an authority from the Jewish chief priests, and he returned with a commission and an authority from heaven that eclipsed any other. He went out in search of Christians to apprehend, and he returned as one who had been apprehended by Christ. He left as one man, and he returned as another. Saul of Tarsus became transformed into Paul the Apostle.

The most noteworthy thing that we learn about Paul is that he experienced a great personal transformation. His Leadership Life was triggered by a momentous occasion when he saw a light and heard a voice from heaven. He had a first-hand encounter with the Lord Jesus Christ. He was profoundly impacted and irrevocably transformed. This became the bedrock of his Leadership Life.

Jesus told Saul that He appeared for the purpose of making Saul into a minister and a witness of the things which would be revealed to him. That certainly made quite an impression, because Saul eventually assumed a new identity as Paul, and before he was martyred, spent the rest of his life preaching and writing the message of Christ. His life became an expression of his revelation. The strength of his Leadership Life arose from the depths of his personal transformation.

I am not suggesting that every leader must first receive a personal visitation from heaven before he or she can become effective. Instead, my point is that dynamic leadership goes beyond merely following a formula or learning a technique. Learning methods and theories is definitely helpful, but there simply is no substitute for a first hand revelation of knowledge. Leaders like Paul make a difference because they live out of realities that others do not. These realities come into view through personal transformation. They experience a powerful inward change, which they carry with them as they serve their world.

The transformative process solidifies what we believe and that for which we are willing to give our lives. Leadership from this vantage point is more than just a job or an obligation, it becomes our life purpose. A transformed life takes our lives from the common approach of passively taking life as it comes into a lively message of, "I've got something worth living for". We shed the unproductive and the unnecessary things, so that we can give ourselves fully to the imperative and the indispensable actions of our purpose. The transformed life moves us into higher dimensions of leadership, where leadership is less about personal success and more about contributing to a greater cause. This type of leadership results when people sense genuine influence rather than the protocol of position and authority. A transformed life produces a leadership that is felt rather than forced.

Jesus reiterated this truth in Matthew 16. He underscored the importance of first-hand revelation and how it serves as the foundation for The Leadership Life:

> When Jesus came into the region of Caesarea Philippi, He asked His disciples, saying, "Who do men say that I, the Son of Man, am?" So they said, "Some say John the Baptist, some Elijah, and others Jeremiah or one of the prophets." He said to them, "But who do you say that I am?" Simon Peter

answered and said, "You are the Christ, the Son of the living God." Jesus answered and said to him, "Blessed are you, Simon Bar-Jonah, for flesh and blood has not revealed this to you, but My Father who is in heaven. And I also say to you that you are Peter, and on this rock I will build My church, and the gates of Hades shall not prevail against it (Matthew 16:13-18).

Peter's first-hand knowledge was something that Jesus said He could build upon that would stand the test of time. Peter was seeing something that the others were seeing, and hearing something that the others were hearing. Deep within, he became aware of who Jesus really was, and this revelation was forever changing who Peter was. Peter's willingness to accept change was commended and his leadership potential was directly linked as an outcome to this process of transformation. People tend to look solely for outward signs of leadership, yet Jesus indicated the value of the inner life in the making of a leader. Transformation occurs from the inside out, and leadership is likewise. A deep and enduring leadership influence emanates from a transformed life. Anything else will prove to be short-term and ill-equipped.

Personal transformation makes such an o impact because it introduces us to our true selves. In the process, we come to an understanding of who we were meant to be, and only then can we become comfortable with walking that out. Our leadership takes on the reflection of this realization. No longer are we searching for who we really are or trying to be something we are not. The best leaders lead by staying true to their authentic selves. They stay submitted to their call and to their vision. Their leadership is more than something they do, it's about who they are. Leadership from this perspective is more about fulfilling a trust and less about achieving personal gain.

Not all people undergo such a dramatic turnaround and conversion experience as Paul did, however, but the principle holds true: A transformed life precipitates the Leadership Life.

A transformed life occurs both in a moment and over a lifetime. What I mean by that is, the process of transformation suddenly begins in a stunning and poignant moment of revelation, but then sets course for a lifetime voyage of personal growth and development. This is the fire we see roaring within Paul. His initial encounter with Christ forever changed him within, but the initial encounter was also an invitation to continually pursue greater discoveries.

I think back to some of my own experiences and how they have altered my course in life. As a college freshman, I began seeking God for direction through prayer and reading the Bible. Alone in my room one night, as I read the Scriptures, it became clear to me that I was lost without Christ. I prayed sincerely from my heart and that was the beginning of my personal transformation. I was changed in a moment, yet the change was not just for the moment. That initial change set me on a path of change; one change led to another.

The process of personal transformation positions us to lead others beyond their current experience. Our newfound perspective sets our course and permeates our leadership. The evidence of living a transformed life will not go unnoticed. People are endowed with an innate sense of purpose, yet they often are not sure what that is supposed to look like. People are searching to find their own way, but they often don't know where to start. When they encounter someone living in the process of transformation, they begin imagining their own possibilities and seeing the way there.

Role models are a priceless commodity at any stage in life; there is something about seeing truth acted out that resonates more clearly than only hearing or reading about it. One reason that role models are so valuable is because they are a rare find. It seems much easier to identify the attributes of strong leadership than it is to locate someone who embodies those desired attributes.

If you ask people about who was most influential in their lives, they will usually point out one or two significant relationships. These encounters became significant because of how they factored into their own personal transformation. We encounter many people throughout life, yet the ones who seem to matter most are the ones who challenge us deep inside to pursue transformation.

We all need teachers. None of us can reach our full potential on our own, yet we cannot live solely on a diet of second hand information. Each of us must also experience some measure of growth through direct reflection and discovery. Let's learn all that we can from all the sources we can, but the concepts and ideas we glean from others must become integrated into our own evolving awareness. Leadership goes beyond just spouting off quotes and quips from our favorite author or following a recommended formula. As we assimilate the learning we must begin to personalize it for ourselves, and then translate it into our own words, actions, and beliefs.

Leadership starts with leading ourselves. That takes more than a knowledge of leadership, it takes the courage to know ourselves and to challenge the status quo. Authentic leadership consists of more than a package of attributes, it is the story of someone who personifies transformation. They have proven they can lead others because they are already leading themselves down the road of growth and change.

The power of a transformed life is found in the ability to pursue change and remove the blinders that hold us back. Transformation breaks barriers and alleviates fears. A transformed life is fueled by the boldness and the ability to ask the right questions. A transformed life requires the courage to sincerely embrace and explore the answers to those questions.

Saul of Tarsus asked two questions that day on the road to Damascus. First he asked, *Who are you Lord?*, and then he asked, *What would you have me to do? (See Acts 22:6-10).*

He received more than he could have imagined in response to both of those questions, and with those answers he also received a transformed life. Paul's transformed life not only benefitted him, but it has influenced countless others ever since. That is the power and the impetus of a transformed life. It becomes a pillar in the formation of The Leadership Life.

The Leadership Life is an impacted life.

The Leadership Life is a surrendered life.

The Leadership is an inside-out life.

The Leadership Life is a transformed life.

> **THE TRANSFORMED LIFE MOVES US INTO HIGHER DIMENSIONS OF LEADERSHIP, WHERE LEADERSHIP IS LESS ABOUT PERSONAL SUCCESS AND MORE ABOUT CONTRIBUTING TO A GREATER CAUSE.**

REVIEW

1. Leadership is the outward evidence of the inner life.
2. There is no substitute for first-hand knowledge derived by revelation.
3. Personal transformation introduces us to our true selves.
4. The best leaders lead from authenticity.
5. Leadership starts with leading ourselves.

REFLECTIONS

1. Do you agree that personal transformation precipitates the Leadership Life? Why or why not?
2. Have you experienced any personal transformations? If so, how has that affected your leadership?
3. What questions are you asking in order to become a better leader?

CHAPTER 7

A TRANSCENDED LIFE

*Therefore, King Agrippa, I was not
disobedient to the heavenly vision
(Acts 26:19).*

Without a doubt, the Apostle Paul lived a life of great influence. One of the most significant sources of his Leadership Life was his complete commitment to a heavenly vision. This is a brief, yet meaningful statement that effectively sums up his approach to life. He chose to live according to the divine encounter he had experienced, and he never looked back. The heavenly vision informed and energized his leadership ability.

Living for a heavenly vision elevates our path from the ordinary to the extraordinary. A heavenly vision raises us above and beyond what we are capable of doing on our own. Our greatness is no longer limited by our personal ability, rather it is linked to the greatness of our cause and the power that God provides. A heavenly vision allows us to surpass and eclipse the boundaries of our natural potential. The Lead-

67

ership Life is a transcended life, because we are living for something and someone greater than ourselves.

I've heard it said that succeeding at something insignificant is not really success, but actually a failure. I have to agree. That outlook makes sense to me because our greatness is only found in God and in our association with Him. There are countless causes that one could choose to live for, but in the end what will matter most?

If we spend our life mastering a skill or devoting ourselves to something that does not serve the purposes of God, we must question its value. If we place our energy and our affection behind something that goes no further than ourselves, we must challenge its worthiness. A transcended life is connected to and driven by something beyond ourselves.

A heavenly vision gets us involved in something larger than life, something that will stretch us and bring out the best in us. A heavenly vision will transcend time, because it is something that existed before we did, and it will continue to live on after we are gone. A heavenly vision aligns our priorities with the heart of God, and infuses life with the vigor of significant purpose.

If we merely live in pursuit of self-serving dreams, we will wind up dissatisfied and unfulfilled because we were made for something much bigger than just ourselves. If we only live for our own entertainment and comfort, we will experience emptiness because we were made to participate in the vision of heaven, which is to reveal the glory of God and to extend the reach of His kingdom. Anything else is less than what we were made to be and do.

Thank God for all the good things we can have and be part of during this life. I'm all for enjoying life and receiving the best of God's blessings, but the truth is that nothing else compares to the depth of fulfillment that accompanies living for a heavenly vision.

Now you may be wondering what I mean by a heavenly vision? I am not saying that everybody has to have a dramatic vision like Paul had, seeing and hearing the Lord Jesus face to face. That kind of experience is certainly more the exception than the rule. What I am referring to is expressed in Proverbs 29:18 which reads, *Where there is no vision, the people perish (cast off restraint).*

All people are wired to operate according to a guiding vision in our hearts, which will direct and carry us through this life. Without the benefit of a positive vision, the result is we are prone to wander aimlessly, searching yet never finding because we don't know what we are looking for. The Bible likens this to sheep without a shepherd. Deep down we sense that there is more to life, but without a healthy vision, our progress is impeded.

Vision is much like attitude: everyone has one, but some are good and some are not. A heavenly vision is something that originates from heaven and that turns our attention to heaven. It causes us to set our affection on things above and not on things below (see Colossians 3:2). A transcended life arises from being connected to a meaningful purpose that lifts us above the shackles of petty pursuits and moves us beyond the confines of small thinking.

A heavenly vision will grab hold of your life, and give you energy and passion that can't be found elsewhere. It sets the course for your life and keeps you focused on the priorities of your heavenly Father. A heavenly vision will expand your thinking and enlarge your perspective. A heavenly vision will sustain you in troubled times and give you courage in the face of seeming impossibilities. A heavenly vision will challenge your ability and demand more than you thought you could give, but in the end it will enrich you more than anything else can.

I like how Paul expressed himself here; he said that he was not disobedient to the heavenly vision. This sounds like Paul made a daily decision to align himself with a guiding vision. Day after day, regardless of external circumstances, Paul was able to be a successful leader because of his faith and commitment to a clear image of future possibilities. This is not just a fleeting fancy or simply daydreaming; this is an embedded and enduring perception that gives definitive direction and shapes strategic thinking.

Vision empowers us with a leadership perspective, which allows us to see beyond the present to navigate toward the desired future. Vision infuses hope, which is a fundamental and necessary element of leadership effectiveness. Leaders are deep thinkers. They are constantly on the lookout for significant signposts that point the way, and they are consistently crafting messages that effectively communicate the why and how of the journey.

Leadership is all about challenging the status quo. This is the definition of a transcended life. Deep within, the leader has already been to places and seen things that go beyond the here and now. They are not ignorant of what the present limitations, yet they are not submissive to them either. Their dreams have carried them further than the reach of time, and they have determined to live today with a view toward tomorrow.

Right now, I am considering the chair I am sitting in right now, and the laptop I am typing on. Both of these things were built from various materials, yet each of them originated with an idea. Someone had a vision to create a tool; in their mind's eye they pictured the end product and found a way to make it happen. This is the same process described by Hebrews 11:1: *Now faith is the substance of things hoped for, the evidence of things not seen.*

Faith is the action that creates the substance of what is hoped for. Vision produces an image of the future one is hoping for, and faith translates the dream into reality. This reminds me of Joshua 1:3, which states, *Every place that the sole of your foot will tread upon I have given you, as I said to Moses.*

God was encouraging Joshua as he prepared to lead Israel into the Promised Land. Basically, God was telling Joshua that he could possess as much of the Promised Land as he was willing to walk out. He would experience victory for as far as he was willing to go with the promise of God.

In much the same way, we can trust God to make His promises substantive in our lives. The vision is the promise of what is hoped for; our response is the action of our faith which results in strategic advances toward tangible change. The image in the heart informs and enacts the potential of the leader. Such is the power of a transcended life.

Paul wrote about this in Philippians 3, in which he recounted the exchange that took place in his life when he turned away from his former ways to seek Christ. He speaks of receiving a press, an urgency and a drive in his heart to reach for the prize of an upward call. I refer to this as a *permanent press*.

Just like an article of clothing, it's an attitude we wear and a mindset we surround ourselves with that impacts our entire being. Living with a permanent press is living with the intentionality and the awareness that proceed from a transcended life. It is a perpetual forward motion based upon the promise that God has more in store for our future.

> *But what things were gain to me, these I have counted loss for Christ. Yet indeed I also count all things loss for the excellence of the knowledge of Christ Jesus my Lord, for whom I have suffered the loss of all things, and count them as rubbish, that I may gain Christ and be found in Him, not having my own righteousness, which is from the law, but that which is through faith in Christ, the righteousness which is from God by faith; that I may know Him and the power of His resurrection, and the fellowship of His sufferings, being conformed to His death, if, by any means, I may attain to the resurrection from the dead. Not that I have already attained, or am already perfected; but I press on, that I may lay hold of that for which Christ Jesus has also laid hold of me. Brethren, I do not count myself to have apprehended; but one thing I do, forgetting those things which are behind and reaching forward to those things which are ahead, I press toward the goal for the prize of the upward call of God in Christ Jesus (Philippians 3:7-14).*

Paul made it clear that he had not yet found his destination. In his heart, he had not yet laid hold of all that was within reach. Yes, he had been transformed, but still there was more.

His transformation repositioned to live a transcended life. From then on, his focus was toward the things ahead and living for the upward call of God.

Receiving a heavenly vision of your own is not as difficult or mysterious as you might imagine. The Bible is the inspired word of God:

> *All Scripture is given by inspiration of God, and is profitable for doctrine, for reproof, for correction, for instruction in righteousness, that the man of God may be complete, thoroughly equipped for every good work (2 Timothy 3:16).*

Leaders are thoroughly equipped to do good works not only through skill, but also with vision and purpose. Readers of the word of God will find the inspiration of a heavenly vision.

The Holy Spirit speaks the language of visions and dreams. Acts 2:16-17 tells us, *And it shall come to pass in the last days, says God, that I will pour out My Spirit on all flesh and your sons and daughters will prophesy and your young men shall see visions and your old men shall dream dreams.* Let the Holy Spirit speak to you, so He can plant heavenly visions and dreams in your heart.

There are many anointed servants of God working diligently to advance the heavenly vision beating in their hearts. If you are not in possession of a heavenly vision that wakes you in the morning and speaks to you through the night, then I suggest you get involved helping someone else with their vision. Talk to your pastor and offer your help, or see how you can support other ministries that are preaching the gospel and meeting people's needs.

Whatever you do, make sure that you

become obedient to a heavenly vision. Live for something bigger than yourself. Live for something that will transcend your lifespan. It is the way of The Leadership Life.

The Leadership Life is a visionary life.

The Leadership Life is an intentional life.

The Leadership Life is a strategic life.

The Leadership Life is a transcended life.

> **A HEAVENLY VISION ALIGNS OUR PRIORITIES WITH THE HEART OF GOD, AND INFUSES LIFE WITH THE VIGOR OF SIGNIFICANT PURPOSE.**

REVIEW

1. Leadership is living for something greater than ourselves.
2. Our greatness is linked to the greatness of our cause.
3. A heavenly vision is something that originates from heaven and turns our attention toward heaven.
4. Leadership is all about challenging the status quo.
5. We are not fully equipped to be leaders without vision and purpose.

REFLECTIONS

1. Is your leadership being driven by a heavenly vision? Explain why or why not.
2. How would you describe the primary purpose behind your leadership?
3. How has God spoken to you in the past about your leadership? How do you plan to continue hearing from Him?

CHAPTER 8

A TRANSPARENT LIFE

*... but declared first to those in
Damascus and in Jerusalem, and
throughout all the region of Judea,
and then to the Gentiles, that they
should repent, turn to God, and do
works befitting repentance
(Acts 26:20).*

The Apostle Paul experienced an extraordinary transformation, and then lived the rest of his life as a passionate communicator of his revelations. Immediately following his encounter on the road to Damascus, Paul began sharing his message of repentance and faith in God at every opportunity. The events of each day became a teaching occasion. He didn't wait for an offer to come; he took the initiative and approached people with his message. Whether he was in the synagogue, in the marketplace, in his home, in his travels, or even in prison, Paul consistently lived a life of transparency, honesty, and openness.

Throughout the pages of the New Testament, we either find Paul standing before an audience and proclaiming his message, seeking and building mentoring relationships, or sharing his thoughts by writing one of his many letters. Clearly, one of his priorities was to serve others by acting as a teaching resource. He lived with an open door policy into his heart. What Paul learned, he as eager to share with others.

Teaching is a leadership responsibility. The Leadership Life is indicative of one who serves through teaching. Leaders are by nature, constant communicators of their perspective. They give direction and they instill their vision. They dialogue with others and they seek to promote understanding. They relate to others and they find ways to invite them into their field of learning.

Leaders seek to add value in every situation through teaching. One of the most basic and authentic leadership behaviors is to reproduce oneself. This requires self-disclosure and generous amounts of personal clarity. People can learn facts from the pages of a book, yet they learn more completely from the pages of our lives.

Genuine leadership focuses on developing more leaders. One of the most effective measures of leadership is not only how many will receive your message, but how many are actually taking your message to others. This is the vital difference between merely helping others acquire knowledge, rather than guiding them through to real-life application of that knowledge.

Leadership is about a call to action, which involves an aspect of teaching. Let's look at several different examples from the Bible that reveal the connection between leadership and teaching.

> *So if you faithfully obey the commands I am giving you today—to love*

the Lord your God and to serve him with all your heart and with all your soul—then I will send rain on your land in its season, both autumn and spring rains, so that you may gather in your grain, new wine and olive oil. I will provide grass in the fields for your cattle, and you will eat and be satisfied. Be careful, or you will be enticed to turn away and worship other gods and bow down to them. Then the Lord's anger will burn against you, and he will shut up the heavens so that it will not rain and the ground will yield no produce, and you will soon perish from the good land the Lord is giving you. Fix these words of mine in your hearts and minds; tie them as symbols on your hands and bind them on your foreheads. Teach them to your children, talking about them when you sit at home and when you walk along the road, when you lie down and when you get up. Write them on the doorframes of your houses and on your gates, so that your days and the days of your children may be many in the land the Lord swore to give your ancestors, as many as the days that the heavens are above the earth (Deuteronomy 11:13-21).

In this passage of Scripture, Moses is giving the people of Israel important directives from the Lord as they prepare to enter the Promised Land. He reminds them that teaching the ways of the Lord to their children must remain a priority. As each generation commits to teaching the next generation, the promised blessings will continue.

I find it interesting how he describes the teaching process. They are encouraged to use every opportunity as teachable moments. Whether they are sitting at home or walking along the road - as part of their morning routine as well as part of their bedtime routine - they are to read, write, and speak the word of the Lord. Throughout the day, as a part of their regular activities, families were given the responsibility to keep the laws of God within range of the eyes and ears of their children. Teaching is a discipline of effective leadership.

In the gospels, we find more examples of how teaching is the ongoing work of leadership.

> *Jesus replied, "Anyone who loves me will obey my teaching. My Father will love them, and we will come to them and make our home with them. Anyone who does not love me will not obey my teaching. These words you hear are not my own; they belong to the Father who sent me. "All this I have spoken while still with you. But the Advocate, the Holy Spirit, whom the Father will send in my name, will teach you all things and will remind you of everything I have said to you (John 14:23-26).*

Jesus accomplished much during His brief, yet powerful earthly ministry. He was known for performing great miracles, but also for His magnificent teaching ability. He taught with unparalleled authority, simplicity, and clarity. He translated profound spiritual truths into common and sensible terms. He took advantage of situations and surroundings to relay answers to some of life's most challenging questions. As He taught, the people followed. Much of His leadership appeal captured hearts through His teaching. Yet His teaching ministry was built on spending time with and among the people.

As Jesus was coming to the end of His life on earth, He spent time preparing His disciples for what was next. For several years, they had accompanied Him as He taught and ministered to people from place to place. Jesus told them about the promised Holy Spirit that would come after Jesus' departure. Just like Jesus, one of the key attributes of the Holy Spirit would be a teaching ministry. A primary function of the Holy Spirit is to be with us at all times, to lead and to guide by teaching us all things. Leadership and teaching both flow from the same motive: to empower and to influence. Teaching is an integrated and interrelated capacity of leadership.

During one of the last encounters the disciples had with Jesus, He gave them what has become known as "The Great Commission." This was the final charge to His followers and encompassed the main focus of His heart. This same commission is still in effect today for you and me.

> *Then Jesus came to them and said, "All authority in heaven and on earth has been given to me. Therefore go and make disciples of all nations, baptizing them in the name of the Father and of the Son and of the Holy Spirit, and teaching them to obey everything I have commanded you. And surely I am with you always, to the very end of the age" (Matthew 28:18-20).*

Jesus gave the command for the church to go in the authority of heaven with one primary objective: to make disciples of all people using the vehicle of teaching. His commission is for the church to lead others into a relationship with Him by teaching them how to obey His commands. This means rubbing shoulders with others, getting to know them, and intertwining our lives with theirs. A successful life is largely dependent upon the benefit of receiving a consistent and correct course of instruction. The value of the instruction is most effective when it comes from a trusted and transparent instructor. This involves more than just a transfer of knowledge; it involves establishing a connection and forming collaboration.

A teaching heart beats within the chest of Jesus. His desire is to sit with us and commune together. As His followers, we are to adopt His approach to the world in which we live. The Apostle Paul recognized this and likewise lived a teaching life. He devoted himself to servant leadership by teaching. His leadership lens is evident in his instruction to Timothy:

> *And the things you have heard me say in the presence of many witnesses entrust to reliable people who will also be qualified to teach others (2 Timothy 2:2).*

The strategy is simple. Teach what you know to those who are willing and able to teach others. In doing so, our leadership effectiveness multiplies. At this point in my life, I have come to the conclusion that I can do more good by what I deposit in the lives of others, rather than what I alone can accomplish. This is the reason that I write: I feel called to express my thoughts, but also because I believe it is a tool to maximize my leadership potential. I am expecting the things I write to contribute to a larger effort of heaven that exceeds my individual ability.

Living a teaching life doesn't necessarily

mean always working out of a classroom setting and preparing official lesson plans. Teaching and learning can take place through different methods. Some people have more of a natural teaching ability than others, but don't allow that to hold you back. Determine to convey your message in a way that is most comfortable and fitting for you.

A teaching life is an intentional and systematic approach to guiding others through the process of learning and discovery. It is a vital function of leadership because it seeks to produce personal growth and long-term change. The Leadership Life wields influence through close proximity and selfless transparency. It extends an invitation to go beyond the superficial, and engenders mutual respect between each party.

The Apostle Paul displayed this by starting where he was after he had a life-changing experience on the road to Damascus. He ended up in the city, recovering from the physical effects of his encounter and coming to grips with his newfound understanding. Several days later, he began to converse with the people of Damascus about his vision.

He didn't wait for an invitation; he simply began sharing his heart with anyone who would listen. He took advantage of his current situation to immediately begin living a life of influence. He had no hesitation becoming transparent and launched into a teaching life that sought to produce a positive and lasting influence on others.

He didn't wait for a whiteboard or for Power Point slides. He didn't wait until he earned a specialized teaching degree from a major university. He didn't wait for the perfect conditions or for the ideal set of circumstances. Although those things are valuable and good, they cannot replace a sincere desire to serve by teaching.

Deep within, Paul was driven by a clear mandate to open his heart and his mouth. The thing that set Paul apart was his passionate approach to teaching. His leadership life was expressed in his dedication to help people discover the truths he had come to know. Our world is a better place because of his decision:

> *For when I preach the gospel, I cannot boast, since I am compelled to preach. Woe to me if I do not preach the gospel (1 Corinthians 9:16).*

Paul didn't talk down on others to prove his intellectual superiority. Instead, he felt compelled to give of his knowledge to others. His experiences and learning were so wonderfully transformational that he could not keep them to himself. Leadership through teaching is not about needing to be heard or gaining a following, but about contributing to a larger cause by empowering and enriching others.

There is a certain vulnerability in living a teaching life. It demands becoming comfortable with being open and transparent with others. By sharing our experiences, our perspectives, and our thoughts, we are inviting people to take a glimpse into our soul. We make ourselves approachable and accessible. We freely give of the best we have to offer: our time and our attention.

This is a true transaction of leadership currency. It's been said that people don't care what you know until they know that you care. A teaching life is up close and personal. We are sharing more than just information; we are sharing a connection. Currency is a medium of exchange, and leadership is similar to currency. By giving transparency, we in return obtain trust and attention from the student. This exchange sets the stage for listening and learning.

Leading by teaching goes beyond just declaring what you know, it is a deeper expression of who you really are. The information alone is valuable and necessary, but to see that same knowledge integrated into the entire package of a person's life is a much greater prize.

When I was in Bible school, I started a window cleaning business to make extra money. On Saturdays, I would clean the windows of a few local businesses. One of the things that I enjoyed most about that was the sense of satisfaction I found in leaving behind a sparkling clear pane of glass. It somehow made me feel good knowing that I had helped the glass more effectively serve its purpose.

Vision is the language of leadership and the power of transparency. It allows the message we embody to be clearly understood. When the glass is dirty, covered in dust and grime, the view is limited and uninviting. But when the glass is clean and clear, the light shines in and the reflection is engaging.

Likewise, our leadership is more successful when the view into our lives is clear and unobstructed. On one hand, a murky and hidden view keeps people at a distance and prevents trust. On the other hand, a commitment to transparency allows free access and generates connection.

The Leadership Life is much like a window. It serves to allow us a perspective from both within and without. When we choose to live with intentionality and transparency, it gives useful insight to others as well as to ourselves. It clarifies our function and helps us to see our potential to effectively meet the needs of others. Concurrently, it reflects honesty and authenticity toward others, which in turn catalyzes leader ship influence.

The Leadership Life of Paul encompassed this type of teaching posture. Those interested in leading will do wisely to follow suit. Both teachers and leaders are interested in achieving long-term benefits by challenging people to set higher goals and to live for greater purposes. Teachers as well as leaders encourage a thirst for learning and exhibit the workings of a strategic mind. A teaching life and a leadership life are both attuned to the similar goal of inspiring personal development regardless of the obstacles. Without a doubt, a teacher is a leader and a leader is a teacher.

The Leadership Life is a teaching life.

The Leadership Life is a communicative life.

The Leadership Life is a relational life.

The Leadership Life is a life of transparency.

> **ONE OF THE MOST EFFECTIVE MEASURES OF LEADERSHIP IS NOT ONLY HOW MANY WILL RECEIVE YOUR MESSAGE, BUT HOW MANY ARE ACTUALLY TAKING YOUR MESSAGE TO OTHERS.**

REVIEW

1. Leaders are constant communicators of their perspective.
2. Leadership is a call to action, which involves an aspect of teaching.
3. Vision is the language of leadership.
4. Transparency reflects honesty and authenticity toward others.
5. Transparency increases the potential for leadership influence.

REFLECTIONS

1. Do you agree that teaching is a leadership responsibility? Why or why not?
2. How have others been influential in your own life through their transparency?
3. In what ways can you begin to live and lead with greater transparency?

CHAPTER 9

A TENACIOUS LIFE

*For these reasons the Jews seized
me in the temple and tried to kill
me (Acts 26:21).*

If there is one characteristic about the Apostle Paul that impresses me more than any other, it is his fierce tenacity. He loved people and served them with compassion. When he encountered challenges, trials, and opposition, however, he stood his ground with the heart of a warrior. He lived with a passionate pursuit of purpose.

The Leadership Life isn't always easy. Along with the victories and successes, there will also be struggles, disappointments, failures, and pain. Not everybody will embrace your ideas, your authority, or your leadership style. In fact, some people may despise you, choose to ignore you, or even feel justified in attacking you. Leaders must be ready for anything, and Paul certainly experienced his share of troubles.

Without question, one of the most necessary and important qualities for living The Leadership Life is a firmness of purpose. There will be challenges to test your resolve each step of the way along your leadership journey. Leadership success doesn't just happen; it emerges from the dogged determination of those who refuse to quit.

An unyielding sense of purpose empowers leadership with clarity, direction, and context. It emphatically answers the question of why you do what you do. It provides energy and sustains effort. It overrides all contrary factors by implanting a personal and perpetual motivation within us.

Years ago, I had the privilege of entering the ministry under the leadership of Dr. Lester Sumrall. He was a spiritual giant, with a legendary faith and a long list of accomplishments. He was not large in physical stature, yet he carried an enormous presence. Near the end of his life, he taught one of his greatest lessons ever, which he entitled "I Did Not Quit". In the message, he recounted many of his contemporaries who for one reason or another, did not finish their race. He wasn't boasting or patting himself on the back; he was reminding us that his ministry success was attributed to one thing above all others: he simply did not quit. He lived a tenacious life.

The dictionary definition of tenacity is *to hold fast, to be persistent in either maintaining or seeking something desired.* A tenacious life exhibits perseverance, endurance, and drive. Some may call it diligence, or moxie, or a strong will. Whichever term you prefer, the underlying meaning remains the same. Success in any endeavor requires a strong dose of tenacity.

In Acts 26, Paul, as he often did, is telling his story. Along with the great adventures, heavenly visions, and marvelous miracles, Paul's Leadership Life was also filled with many difficulties. The Jewish religious leaders vehemently opposed him, and sought to take his life on several occasions. Eventually, after an extended prison term, Paul was martyred for his faith in Rome.

Through it all, Paul refused to back away from his purpose. He maintained a big- picture view of life, which kept him going through the daily grind. Look at the daunting list of challenges he faced.

> I have worked much harder, been in prison more frequently, been flogged more severely, and been exposed to death again and again. Five times I received from the Jews the forty lashes minus one. Three times I was beaten with rods, once I was pelted with stones, three times I was shipwrecked, I spent a night and a day in the open sea, and I have been constantly on the move. I have been in danger from rivers, in danger from bandits, in danger from my fellow Jews, in danger from Gentiles; in danger in the city, in danger in the country, in danger at sea; and in danger from false believers. I have labored and toiled and have often gone without sleep; I have known hunger and thirst and have often gone without food; I have been cold and naked. Besides everything else, I face daily the pressure of my concern for all the churches (2 Corinthians 11:23-28).

I am not suggesting that all leaders will experience the same level of persecution and punishment to which Paul was subjected. The point is that Paul's leadership influence became so powerful in large part to his willingness to stay the course. He was sold out to his cause, and he was determined to either fulfill his mission or to die trying.

The Leadership Life can be painful at times, yet those who learn how to respond effectively in the midst of it reach their leadership potential. When we live for a mission that is bigger than ourselves, it enlarges us from within and increases our tolerance level. It ignites a fire in our being and releases a spiritual stamina that empowers us to go the distance. The comfort of knowing we are serving a higher purpose sustains us through the discomforts we may face along the way.

Some of the best leadership advice I've ever heard was summed up in these few words: Don't allow yourself to get bitter. People may do you wrong, and plans may fall flat. Promises may get broken, and your best efforts may not seem to be enough. Sometimes you may get discouraged, wondering if it's really worth it all, or if anyone really cares. Come what may, decide to get better rather than to get bitter. Your Leadership Life depends on it.

The Apostle Paul is still an example of exceptional leadership today because he lived with a mindset that his endurance would be rewarded. The vision in his heart overshadowed the pain of his outward circumstances. He lived focused on making a contribution and leaving a legacy. He was driven by a sense of urgency that lifted him above the trials and troubles surrounding him. He is long gone, yet his influence continues. The Leadership Life is fueled by the power of tenacity.

Of course, Paul's leadership was empowered by the Spirit of Christ. He recognized and celebrated the grace of God that enabled his life. Thankfully, that same relentless hope and can-do attitude are available to us as well. The same

Spirit that buoyed Paul's Leadership Life many years ago is still at work in lives today. The following are a few Scripture references that help explain the driving force within Paul's heart.

> But by the grace of God I am what I am, and his grace to me was not without effect. No, I worked harder than all of them--yet not I, but the grace of God that was with me (1 Corinthians 15:10).

> Therefore, my dear brothers and sisters, stand firm. Let nothing move you. Always give yourselves fully to the work of the Lord, because you know that your labor in the Lord is not in vain (1 Corinthians 15:58).

> However, I consider my life worth nothing to me; my only aim is to finish the race and complete the task the Lord Jesus has given me—the task of testifying to the good news of God's grace (Acts 20:24).

> Endure suffering along with me, as a good soldier of Christ Jesus (2 Timothy 2:3).

> For I can do everything through Christ, who gives me strength (Philippians 4:13).

A tenacious life is not a self-reliant or a self-sufficient life. It is not proving yourself or looking to showcase your own abilities. Rather, it arises from a sober and humble recognition of the call of God to participate in His grand design. The tenacity of the Leadership Life is activated in a heart that trusts in Him to show Himself strong on our behalf and to remain faithful to His promises. A tenacious life is fueled by faith and hope in what lies ahead rather than what lies within. Our confidence comes from knowing that we have a place in God's purposes, not from trying to obtain His blessing upon our purposes.

Hope is an unstoppable and irrepressible force. It's been said that people can live for only a few weeks without food, only a few days without water, only a few minutes without oxygen, but they cannot live at all without hope. The hope of salvation, the hope of Israel, and the hope of the resurrection are the things that kept Paul afloat in a sea of distress. The hope of making a difference, the hope of a better future, and the hope of goals being accomplished are the things that energize The Leadership Life by generating tremendous tenacity and resiliency.

The writer of Hebrews gave us something to think about regarding the example that Jesus left for us.

> *Therefore, since we are surrounded by such a great cloud of witnesses, let us throw off everything that hinders and the sin that so easily entangles. And let us run with perseverance the race marked out for us, fixing our eyes on Jesus, the pioneer and perfecter of faith. For the joy set before him he endured the cross, scorning its shame, and sat down at the right hand of the throne of God. Consider him who endured such opposition from sinners, so that you will not grow weary and lose heart (Hebrews 12:1-3).*

In order to help us finish our race, we are instructed to consider how Jesus endured the incomprehensible suffering and separation from the Father at the cross. He endured a violent and hateful opposition. He endured a shameful and torturous death. He endured the wrath of God on our behalf and spent three days separated from heaven. He found strength to endure such monumental pressure by focusing on the joy that was set before Him. His hope in the promises and purposes of God carried Him through His darkest hours. We are encouraged to do the same, lest we grow weary and lose heart.

David, under the inspiration of the Holy Spirit, wrote of this in the Psalms many centuries earlier. He is writing of his own experience, yet he is also prophesying about Jesus and the challenges He would face. Through David's words, we are granted some insight into the heart and mind of Jesus as He walks through the agony of bearing the burden of the cross.

> I keep my eyes always on the LORD. With him at my right hand, I will not be shaken. Therefore my heart is glad and my tongue rejoices; my body also will rest secure, because you will not abandon me to the realm of the dead, nor will you let your faithful one see decay. You make known to me the path of life; you will fill me with joy in your presence, with eternal pleasures at your right hand (Psalm 16:8-11).

Here we learn that Jesus overcame His difficulties by keeping His focus on the promises of God. He was not moved away from His purpose by keeping His attention fixed on the Lord. His heart was glad and His tongue rejoiced, even in the midst of suffering, knowing the faithfulness of His Father's promise to raise Him from the grave. His mission required great sacrifice, yet He stayed the course with joy and peace. His security was found in His adherence to the significance and the source of His mission.

I like to call this *a marathon mindset*. It equips the Leadership Life with a greater capacity to perform. Just as the runner must breathe well to continue the race, leaders must think well to navigate their way. Effective leadership starts with managing our own thoughts and dispelling our own doubts. With each breath, the runner is replenished by expelling the stale air and receiving fresh air. The process is simple, yet absolutely essential.

Similarly, the Leadership Life must develop a rhythm of discarding thoughts that de-energize and replacing them with thoughts that re-energize. Romans 12:2 calls this *renewing our minds*. It is a continual process of avoiding introspection that causes resistance, and concentrating instead on the promises of God. Running our race works better when we decide to remove the things that hinder, and decide to stay focused on the things that inspire forward motion. The source of energy is found beyond ourselves, and is rooted in our understanding of the larger plan and purpose for which we exist.

Likewise, we can walk through the most difficult of times with tenacious hope, knowing the certainty of our cause. We cannot be overcome because our cause cannot be overcome. The Leadership Life emerges from those who choose to live a life of sacrifice in expectation of greater returns. The Leadership Life is about living selflessly with a tenacious sense of mission. The Leadership Life grows out of hearts that surrender to purpose. We don't decide our own purposes, we surrender to them. We don't make them happen, they make us. Like an escalator, it lift us higher and take us further, but first it requires our cooperation and our surrender.

My parents have modeled this type of leadership throughout my life. Surviving the rigors and the dangers of the World War II, they afterward immigrated to America from Italy. They worked tirelessly and lived sacrificially, raising four children and always sharing their goods with those in need. Like many others, they came to America with a dream of building a better life, and in the process they contributed immensely to society as exemplary citizens. Their dream of a better life wasn't only for personal gain or comfort; it was also for the benefit of the next generation. They live tenaciously in support of others.

That is the spirit of The Leadership Life - to live for something beyond yourself, and to do so graciously and joyfully. Living for a worthy cause will always bring challenges, and will require sacrifice. The Leadership Life draws on strength found in the larger purpose of the mission to which we are called. We fight the good fight of faith, confident in the surety and validity of the cause. Our confidence grows in proportion to our sense of mission, which then bolsters our tenacity.

The Leadership Life is a hopeful life.

The Leadership Life is a relentless life.

The Leadership Life is a self-sacrificing life.

The Leadership Life is a life lived with tenacity.

> **SUCCESS IN ANY ENDEAVOR REQUIRES
> A STRONG DOSE OF TENACITY.**

REVIEW

1. A tenacious life is built upon a firmness of purpose.
2. Tenacity is defined as being persistent in either maintaining or seeking something desired.
3. Choose to get better rather than to get bitter.
4. Leadership depends on a mindset that your endurance will be rewarded.
5. A marathon mindset equips leadership ability with a sense of mission.

REFLECTION

1. Are you living with a passionate pursuit of purpose? How so?
2. What strategies have you found to be effective when you are struggling with discouragement?
3. In what ways can you intensify your level of tenacity?

CHAPTER 10

A THANKFUL LIFE

*Therefore, having obtained help
from God, to this day I stand,
witnessing both to small and great,
saying no other things than those
which the prophets and Moses said
would come: that the Christ would
suffer, that He would be the first
to rise from the dead, and would
proclaim light to the Jewish people,
and to the Gentiles
(Acts 26:22-23).*

We now come to the culmination of Paul's story. As he recounted his way of life in response to the questioning of King Agrippa, Paul ended his discourse with a summation of his Leadership Life. The story began with the impact of his transformation experience, which led to a transcending and a transparent way of life. From there, we learned of Paul's tenacity in the midst of many troubles and trials. Finally, we come to understand one more crucial characteristic in the formation of such an outstanding life of influence.

It is evident that Paul lived a thankful life.

He gave credit to God for helping him along the way, and in the process he explained one of the primary motivators that compelled his leadership. Paul recognized the enormous goodness of God that surrounded his life, and he was driven to share it with others. He was thankful for how much had been granted to him, and it stimulated a powerful life of service and leadership.

Gratitude is often an unnoticed and unheralded aspect of good leadership. Too often, leaders fall prey to the natural tendency of a self-centered mentality. Their leadership is all about them and what they want. At times, their focus on getting things done keeps them from seeing the bigger picture. This approach is common, yet the most effective leadership comes from a different perspective.

An outlook filtered through gratitude allows us to see what is good and what is right about life, and builds a desire within to give back. By acknowledging the help that we have received, we prevent self-absorption and we extract meaning from our experiences. Thankfulness and appreciation creates personal change, which feeds our leadership influence.

The Leadership Life is founded on the principle of stewardship. A thankful life is centered in the belief that we are entrusted with innate gifts, tools, and opportunities for doing the greatest good. Leaders recognize that an important part of their role is to promote long-term sustainability for the mission of their organization. They give of themselves as those being held responsible to further the cause.

Stewardship is not about control, but rather about care. Leadership is dedication to taking care of business, not only for profit or recognition, but to serve the core values of the organization. This begins by recognizing the opportunity to make a worthwhile contribution.

Gratitude sees potential in every situation, and inspires the achievement of great possibilities. It is a source of energy and well-being, which prompts virtue and action. Thankful leaders are resilient, relational, and generous.

A thankful life is lived intentionally, with a freedom that eludes others. It causes us to ask healthy questions and to develop positive insights. It neutralizes the negative influences that assail us, and raises us to greater heights of moral aptitude. Thankfulness enjoys what has been and builds belief in what is still possible. When we look back on where we have come from, and how we got from there to here, our image of the future improves. We understand our connection to a larger purpose, and we gain confidence to continue what we started. Living thankfully today sets in motion the building blocks for a better tomorrow.

As we read through the New Testament writings of Paul, it is evident that he typically started and ended his letters with a theme of thanksgiving. Again and again, He expressed thanks for the love and mercy of God, for his partners and friends, and for the privilege of being part of the work of the Lord. His leadership influence flowed from a deep understanding of the abundance in his life. It was from that awareness that he was motivated to serve and to live abundantly for others.

> *Let me say first that I thank my God through Jesus Christ for all of you, because your faith in him is being talked about all over the world. God knows how often I pray for you. Day and night I bring you and your needs in prayer to God, whom I serve with all my heart*

by spreading the Good News about his Son. One of the things I always pray for is the opportunity, God willing, to come at last to see you. For I long to visit you so I can bring you some spiritual gift that will help you grow strong in the Lord. When we get together, I want to encourage you in your faith, but I also want to be encouraged by yours. I want you to know, dear brothers and sisters, that I planned many times to visit you, but I was prevented until now. I want to work among you and see spiritual fruit, just as I have seen among other Gentiles. For I have a great sense of obligation to people in both the civilized world and the rest of the world, to the educated and uneducated alike. So I am eager to come to you in Rome, too, to preach the Good News (Romans 1:8-15).

In this passage, Paul revealed that his eagerness and sense of obligation to preach the gospel were rooted in gratitude. He gave thanks for the church at Rome and for the opportunity to serve them. He declared that he was filled with a sense of indebtedness, wanting to give back to others because of the wealth of his own experiences. Being thankful opens our eyes toward the presence, the importance, and needs of others.

In his letter to the Ephesians, we see similar language emanating from Paul's pen. He starts off with thanks, not just for his own things, but for other people and how they are growing through his leadership and example. Then he expresses his passion to see them continue growing.

Ever since I first heard of your strong faith in the Lord Jesus and your love for God's people everywhere, I have not stopped thanking God for you. I pray for you constantly, asking God, the glorious Father of our Lord Jesus Christ, to give you spiritual wisdom and insight so that you might grow in your knowledge of God (Ephesians 1:15-17).

Once again, in his usual fashion, we see the same ideas in Paul's letter to the Colossians. He begins by giving thanks for the people who have been influenced by his leadership, and then he encourages them that the appropriate response to an understanding of the goodness of God, is to consistently live with joy and thanks. This was Paul's manner, and this was Paul's Leadership Life:

We always thank God, the Father of our Lord Jesus Christ, when we pray for you, because we have heard of your faith in Christ Jesus and of the love you have for all God's people— the faith and love that spring from the hope stored up for you in heaven and about which you have already heard in the true message of the gospel that has come to you. In the same way, the gospel is bearing fruit and growing throughout the whole world—just as it has been doing among you since the day you heard it and truly understood God's grace. You learned it from Epaphras, our dear fellow servant, who is a faithful minister of Christ on our behalf, and who also told us of your love in the Spirit. For this reason, since the day we heard about you, we have

103

not stopped praying for you. We continually ask God to fill you with the knowledge of his will through all the wisdom and understanding that the Spirit gives, so that you may live a life worthy of the Lord and please him in every way: bearing fruit in every good work, growing in the knowledge of God, being strengthened with all power according to his glorious might so that you may have great endurance and patience, and giving joyful thanks to the Father, who has qualified you to share in the inheritance of his holy people in the kingdom of light. For he has rescued us from the dominion of darkness and brought us into the kingdom of the Son he loves, in whom we have redemption, the forgiveness of sins (Colossians 1:3-14).

It's been said that gratitude is the parent virtue. All other virtues, such as kindness, compassion, and generosity, seem to originate from a thankful heart. When we acknowledge and appreciate that we are the beneficiaries of the grace of God and the help of others, it positions us to live effectively. It encourages us to live respectfully and responsibly creating an internal environment of confident humility. We approach life with greater degrees of purpose, respect, and graciousness.

The same is true with The Leadership Life. Gratitude generates and activates leadership behavior. A thankful attitude makes us happier, healthier, and more inspirational. Living with a genuine perspective of gratitude enables us to add value to others, to discern meaning in every situation, and to bring energy into the demands of each day. Living thankfully brings out the best in us, which then helps us to bring out the best in others.

Let's examine another portion of Scripture that reveals Paul's mindset:

> *This, then, is how you ought to regard us: as servants of Christ and as those entrusted with the mysteries God has revealed. Now it is required that those who have been given a trust must prove faithful. I care very little if I am judged by you or by any human court; indeed, I do not even judge myself. My conscience is clear, but that does not make me innocent. It is the Lord who judges me. Therefore judge nothing before the appointed time; wait until the Lord comes. He will bring to light what is hidden in darkness and will expose the motives of the heart. At that time each will receive their praise from God. Now, brothers and sisters, I have applied these things to myself and Apollos for your benefit, so that you may learn from us the meaning of the saying, "Do not go beyond what is written." Then you will not be puffed up in being a follower of one of us over against the other. For who makes you different from anyone else? What do you have that you did not receive? And if you did receive it, why do you boast as though you did not? (1 Corinthians 4:1-7).*

Clearly, Paul was motivated by the understanding that he had received great things from heaven: great revelations, great responsibilities, and great opportunities. Above all else, his driving force was to be a faithful steward with the call of God. He did not live for other people's approval, but rather for the Lord's pleasure. He was loyal, committed, and unselfish. He did not crave people's attention for himself, yet he was eager to stand up and be heard. He did not think of himself as better than others, yet he set a high standard in all that he did. These are the characteristics of a thankful life. These are the attributes of one grateful to serve the purposes of God. This is the heart of the Leadership Life.

The psalmist makes a valuable distinction between those seeking to live a successful life and those who don't. When we live with an appreciation of all that has been bestowed upon us, we tap into a flow of strength and stability. It protects us from becoming small-minded, insecure, needy, and greedy. The pressures of life can move people off purpose, causing them to grow increasingly discontented and distracted. When we allow worry and unhealthy self-interest to govern our lives, we become misguided and ineffective. A grateful attitude helps to guard against the scorn and contempt that sometimes poisons people. Here is what the psalmist has to say:

> *Blessed is the man who walks not in the counsel of the ungodly, nor stands in the path of sinners, nor sits in the seat of the scornful; but his delight is in the law of the Lord, and in His law he meditates day and night. He shall be like a tree planted by the rivers of water, that brings forth its fruit in its season, whose leaf also shall not wither; and whatever he does shall prosper (Psalm 1:1-3).*

By meditating on the Word of God, we find delight and are refreshed. As we discover the wealth of blessing that God has extended toward us, we are lifted into a broader and better view of ourselves and of others. Our lives become richer as our hearts grow larger and our vision becomes clearer. We become rooted and vibrant, filled with a life that produces good fruit for the benefit of others. We find enthusiasm rather than stagnation, and we reach for greater potential.

When God called Abraham, He gave him a two-sided promise:

> Now the Lord had said to Abram: "Get out of your country, from your family and from your father's house, to a land that I will show you. I will make you a great nation; I will bless you and make your name great; and you shall be a blessing. I will bless those who bless you, and I will curse him who curses you; and in you all the families of the earth shall be blessed" (Genesis 12:1-3).

He was called into blessing so that he would become a blessing. The same applies to you and me. We are called into blessing, not only to enjoy for ourselves, but to carry that blessing further into the future. Too often, people eagerly pursue the blessing, yet they do not comprehend that the promise is only complete when we appreciate its depth and then take it to others.

As I write this, we are entering the Memorial Day weekend. To some it is just a long weekend that marks the start of the summer season. The true meaning is to set aside a time to remember the sacrifices of our military families and to honor their service in our behalf. The freedoms we enjoy as American citizens were secured and defended by their dedicated service and sacrifice. Living in appreciation of such examples of courage and morality empowers our ability to choose paths that make a difference for others.

Gratitude releases us from our insecurities so that we can become our best selves. We are not truly qualified to lead others until we learn to lead ourselves. Leading ourselves involves learning to live with gratitude. Thankful lives are more conscious and caring of others, more mature and dependable. Grateful people are more relational and respectful. All those are qualities of The Leadership Life.

The Leadership Life is a reflective life.

The Leadership Life is an appreciative life.

The Leadership Life is an engaged life.

The Leadership Life is a thankful life.

> **THANKFULNESS ENJOYS WHAT HAS BEEN AND BUILDS BELIEF IN WHAT IS STILL POSSIBLE.**

REVIEW

1. Gratitude stimulates a life of service and leadership.
2. The Leadership Life is founded on the principle of stewardship.
3. Thankfulness motivates us to live abundantly toward others.
4. Gratitude is the parent virtue.
5. Gratitude activates leadership behavior.

REFLECTIONS

1. For what are you most thankful? How does that influence your leadership?
2. Do you agree that gratitude is the parent virtue? Why or why not?
3. In what ways can you begin to live a more thankful life?

CONCLUSION

I hope this book has caused you to think more about your leadership. Yes, you are a leader, and yes, you can make a difference. Get that settled once and for all, so you can move forward on the path God has prepared for you. God has gifted you with something good, and your leadership path is to identify that ability and to begin sharing it with the world.

In conclusion, I want to leave you with one more question. My observation is that the best answers in life seem to come to those who ask the best questions. So here is my question: Will you lead?

My questions only contains three words, but a great deal is wrapped up in those three words. I didn't ask, *can* you lead, or *should* you lead, or *do* you lead? My question is, *will* you lead?

That's because leadership is a choice. It is our response to the call of duty. It is your reply to the heartbeat of God for this generation as David had for his day: *For David, after he had served the purpose of God in his own generation, fell asleep (Acts 13:36).*

Like David, let's step up and live The Leadership Life. Whether you are already leading in some capacity, or if you are wrestling with the

111

concept of leadership, choose to live The Leadership Life.

Jesus told His disciples, *You did not choose me, but I chose you and appointed you so that you might go and bear fruit (John 15:16).* Those words apply to us today just as much as they did to the original disciples many years ago.

Like many others who have come before you, the Lord is extending an invitation to serve His purposes and to leave a legacy of leadership. Whoever you are and wherever you are, you are called to serve God's purposes in your generation. You are chosen and appointed for The Leadership Life. There is specific fruit assigned for your life, the fruit of your labors, which will not manifest without your cooperation. Psalm 110:3 reads, *Your people shall be willing in the day of your power…*

Will you lead? *Will* you accept the call? *Will* you be a willing vessel during the lifetime of God's power in you? Will you leave a faith footprint?

In John 6:9 we find what I refer to as a faith footprint: *"There's a young boy here with five barley loaves and two fish. But what good is that with this huge crowd?"* There were thousands of hungry people in that place, and Jesus wanted to feed them all. The problem was that they didn't have any food to give them. That's when we find out about a young boy with a small lunch of fish and bread.

The Bible doesn't exactly indicate whether the boy volunteered his lunch or not, but I believe that he stepped up and offered what he had. He was willing in the day of God's power to do what he could do. It didn't seem like much, but in the hands of Jesus it went a long way. Everyone had plenty to eat, and with much to spare.

This tells us that leadership doesn't always come from the smartest one in the room. It doesn't always come from the most talented, best educated, or most likely to succeed. Now all of those things are great and there's nothing wrong with them. It's just that without a willing vessel, their potential for good is wasted.

We don't know the boy's name or anything else about him. Yet for all of eternity, he left a faith footprint. He lived a leadership moment, and The Leadership Life is simply a continuous series of leadership moments.

That's why I ask, *will* you lead? Don't be dismayed by thinking that the best you can do is the equivalent of a fish sandwich. Don't be distracted by thinking that your contribution is so small compared to the enormous needs of your fellow man. What you have to offer may not seem like it can do much good, but when you place it in the hands of Jesus, great things can happen.

I'll leave you with this. One of my favorite movies is *Saving Private Ryan*. I greatly admire and have the utmost respect for people willing to sacrifice themselves for a cause they believe in.

In the movie, a unit is tasked with finding Private Ryan so he can return home. His other three brothers have already been killed in action, and the U.S. government doesn't want this family to suffer the loss of all four of their sons.

They finally located Private Ryan, but a fierce battle ensued before he headed for home. As the leader of the unit was wounded and bleeding to death, he pulled Private Ryan up close and told him, "Earn this." In other words, he was telling Private Ryan to go back and live a life worthy of the price that was paid to rescue him.

We can draw such a powerful parallel for yourself from that scene. I'm not talking about earning God's mercy and salvation, for those are gifts of His grace (see Ephesians 2:8-9). Rather, I am referring to living a life worthy of the price that was paid to give you a life to live. If all you live for is personal pleasure and comfort, you will end up disappointed and dissatisfied, because you were made for so much more.

Step up and choose to live The Leadership Life. It is a life of:

- conviction, revealing the truth of God;
- character, revealing the nature of God;
- competence, revealing the power of God;
- consistency, revealing the image of God;
- compassion, revealing the essence of God.

The Leadership Life is:

- a transformed life, revealing the majesty of God;
- a transcended life, revealing the greatness of God;
- a transparent life, revealing the holiness of God;
- a tenacious life, revealing the persistence of God;
- a thankful life, revealing the graciousness of God.

The Leadership Life is a meaningful life.

The Leadership Life is an influential life.

The Leadership Life is a life lived for the purposes of God.

Live The Leadership Life.

MY PRAYER FOR YOU

My prayer is that you will experience all that God has planned for your life. That includes receiving Jesus Christ as your personal Lord and Savior. If you haven't done that yet, please use the following prayer to make that decision right now.

Lord Jesus, thank You for Your sacrifice on the cross to save me from my sins. I repent of my sins and I accept Your gift of forgiveness and eternal life. By faith, I receive You now as my eternal Lord and Savior. Teach me how to live for You for the rest of my life. Amen.

About the Author

John Merola is dedicated to helping people experience the life-changing power of the Lord Jesus Christ. His travelling ministry brings a message of passion, power, and purpose to churches across the country. His focus is to inspire people with a passion for others, the power of faith, and a purpose for life.

John has many years of ministerial experience in a variety of roles. He has served in helps ministry, youth ministry, as an associate pastor, and as an evangelist. He first received ordination to ministry under Dr. Lester Sumrall, and later graduated from Rhema Bible Training Center in Broken Arrow, OK. He holds a graduate degree in Organizational Leadership from Geneva College and, in addition to his ministry travels, he serves as the Director of Empower - NBCA School of Ministry.

He and his wife Lori have three sons. For more information or to contact John for a speaking engagement please visit his ministry website at www.johnmerola.org.

www.ingramcontent.com/pod-product-compliance
Lightning Source LLC
Chambersburg PA
CBHW072027040426
42447CB00009B/1773